Praise for
Lead Like a PIRATE

"If you're ready to take your school or district to the next level of excellence, you need to read *Lead Like a PIRATE*. Shelley Burgess and Beth Houf share personal stories and expert advice on how to build and lead a crew—and how to create a culture where each crew member is valued. They offer the perfect mix of inspiration, encouragement, and real-world experience to help you become the kind of leader you have always wanted to be."

—Todd Whitaker, professor of Educational Leadership,
University of Missouri

"When you read *Lead Like a PIRATE*, you will understand that you are not alone. The authors discuss the ups and downs of leadership in an authentic and compelling way, while helping you steer your direction and the direction of your organization to a much better path. Fun, easy to read, authentic, and packed with ideas to do right now, this is a great book for any leader who is passionate about moving themselves and others forward."

—George Couros, author of *The Innovator's Mindset*

"Based on undeniable experience, brilliance, and heart, *Lead Like A PIRATE* is a book that will push you to think, reflect, and go for greatness. Staying true to PIRATE, Beth Houf and Shelley Burgess creatively unfold the acronym with their own unique twist, revealing what leading should look like in every school. Packed with stories, practical tools and strategies, thought-provoking challenges, and a message so clearly fueled by passion, Beth and Shelley will connect to you as the genuine leaders they are. Regardless of your title, *Lead Like a PIRATE* will inspire you to lead in your own way, brainstorm ideas to up your game, and take risks in influencing others around you, because it's the right thing to do. A text that holds empowerment, world-changing practices, and immense potential for positive change, *Lead Like a PIRATE* should be in the hands of every educator across the globe."

—Nili Bartley, technology integration specialist

"As a big fan of *Teach Like a PIRATE*, I was thrilled to know Beth and Shelley were writing this book for leaders. And they did not disappoint. The book has all the energy, excitement, and enthusiasm you would expect. Having this book is like having a personal coach in your corner. You'll be on your way to better leadership and a stronger school."
—David Geurin, 2017 NASSP Digital Principal of the Year

"Beth and Shelley lay down the gauntlet in *Lead Like a PIRATE* and truly effuse the message of passion from their hearts. They are unwavering in their excitement for creating truly exceptional schools that all kids will want to be running into each and every day! *Lead Like a PIRATE* is a must-read book and will sharpen your sword and thrust you into the battle for doing what's best for kids!"
—Adam Welcome, co-author of *Kids Deserve It*,
director of innovation and technology

"In *Lead Like a PIRATE*, Shelley and Beth provide us with a road map for finding our passion for leadership and service. Every school leader and aspiring administrator who wants to begin the journey of making a difference (rather than focusing on compliance) should read this book. PIRATE leaders need more crew and fewer passengers. I am on board!"
—Salome Thomas-EL, award-winning teacher, principal, and author

"As an enthusiastic future administrator, I have found my treasure map and my treasure chest overflowing with gems! *Lead Like a PIRATE* contains a plethora of practical ideas and strategies to keep the PIRATE culture alive while captaining the ship. Not only do Shelley and Beth provide insight into their leadership experiences, but they also give the PIRATE leader a compass to help navigate the administrative roles while embracing their unique talents to create 'a school culture where students and staff are running to get in and not out.' I'm honored to own this abundance of wealth before stepping into administration. Watch out world; this girl WILL *Lead Like a PIRATE*!"
—Tara Martin, curriculum facilitator, Lawrence Public Schools, USD 497

"Every so often a book comes along that actually reads you. No matter where you are at in your school-leadership journey, Shelley and Beth will help propel you to greatness. These pages contain an enchanted comingling of inspiration and pragmatic ideas. You will feel your leadership capacity increase while reading *Lead Like a PIRATE*."

—Dr. Brad Gustafson, National Distinguished Principal and author of
Renegade Leadership

"Shelley Burgess and Beth Houf take PIRATE leadership to new depths in *Lead Like a PIRATE*. This book shows that courageous leaders can build the types of schools where adults are excited to work and kids are excited to come to school. Beth and Shelley have taken their experiences in educational leadership and drawn a treasure map toward success for those of us who aspire to be great. This book will take you out of your comfort zone and push you toward greatness. The challenges, which are included throughout the book, will push you to become a better leader. Like the other PIRATE books before it (*Teach Like A PIRATE*, *Learn Like A PIRATE*, *Play Like A Pirate*, and *Explore Like A Pirate*,) I will continually go back to *Lead Like a PIRATE* when I need inspiration, motivation, and ideas that will make my school better."

—Jay Billy, principal, Slackwood Elementary School

"Reading *Lead Like a PIRATE* is like sharing a cup of coffee with two upbeat and positive mentors at an EdCamp. Shelley Burgess and Beth Houf share relatable anecdotes from their respective leadership journeys and weave a book that will serve as a passionate addition to any educator's bookshelf. More than that, the dynamic duo of Burgess and Houf provides a blueprint filled with actionable ideas, clear resources, and invitational reflective questions for compassionate leadership in the schoolhouse. A game-changing book written in service and support of students, educators, and school communities, *Lead Like a PIRATE* will ignite the inspiration for the PIRATE leader within all of us."

—Sean Gaillard, former principal, Buncee education advisor,
and founder of #CelebrateMonday

"*Lead Like a PIRATE* is a must-read for those leaders who are looking to transform their leadership, create a positive working and learning environment, and build amazing learning experiences for kids and adults. This book needed to be written. It provides a compass to sail the choppy waters of educational leadership and the treasure map to guide leaders to find the gold within their schools and themselves!"

—Mandy Ellis, principal and lead learner at Dunlap Grade School

"Shelley and Beth have put their hearts and souls on the pages of this book. I still remember the day I read *Teach Like a PIRATE* and the impact the book instantly had on my teaching career. As I read through *Lead Like a PIRATE*, I had that same feeling all over again as a campus administrator. Coming from two who have been through the trenches, I could feel the passion and honesty on every page. This book is one that I will be re-reading time and time again."

—Todd Nesloney, award-winning educator, author, and international speaker

"Every educator, regardless of their title, has within them the capacity to lead and to make a positive impact on the students they serve. Burgess and Houf remind us in *Lead Like a PIRATE* that leaders must embrace the notion that their primary role is culture first, culture next, culture always. Drawing from their extensive educational experiences, these two passionate authors share a number of dynamic examples and strategies that will invigorate you and leave you feeling inspired to create amazing learning experiences for all kids!"

—Jimmy Casas, senior fellow, International Center for Leadership in Education, author, speaker

LEAD
Like a
PIRATE

Make School Amazing for Your Students and Staff

By
Shelley Burgess & Beth Houf

Lead Like a PIRATE

© 2017 by Shelley Burgess and Beth Houf

This book is available at special discounts when purchased in quantity for use as premiums, promotions, fundraisers, or for educational use. For inquiries and details, contact the publisher at shelley@daveburgessconsulting.com.

Published by Dave Burgess Consulting, Inc.
San Diego, CA
http://daveburgessconsulting.com

Cover Design by Genesis Kohler
Editing and Interior Design by My Writers' Connection

Library of Congress Control Number: 2017935677
Paperback ISBN: 978-1-946444-00-4
Ebook ISBN: 978-1-946444-01-1
Hardcover ISBN: 978-1-946444-19-6
First Printing: March 2017

Dedication

We dedicate this book to each person who has made a difference in our lives. All pirate captains need a crew and we have been blessed to be surrounded by the best!

To Our Families

You have been there for us always. Through the early mornings and late nights, the exhaustion and the crazy. You have loved us, encouraged us, and supported us so that we can be the best educators possible.

To Our Students, Staff, Colleagues, and Mentors

You have made us better. You have believed in us, pushed us, challenged us . . . and we are forever grateful. We are the leaders we are because of you!

To Our PLN

You have raised the bar for us. You have connected with us, shared with us, learned with us, and helped us grow. You have increased the caliber of our work and inspired us on a daily basis.

To our Editor, Cover Designer, and Book Team

You have made our vision a reality. You have elevated our work to a new level. Our words have found a voice because of you. Thank you for helping us to share it with the world!

CONTENTS

Foreword xi
The Story of Us xiii
Introduction xvii

Section I: Lead Like a PIRATE 1

1 Passion 2
2 Immersion 14
3 Rapport 28
4 Ask & Analyze 44
5 Transformation 54
6 Enthusiasm 66

Section II: X Marks the Spot: Leadership Treasure.......73

7 Set Your Compass 75
8 Avoid the Blame Game 81
9 Harness the Power of Teams 85
10 Find the Magic in the People—Not Programs 93
11 Get the Right People on the Ship 99
12 If It's Important ... Make Time for It. 103
13 Make Changes without Capsizing Your Ship 107
14 Use Stories to Personalize Data 115
15 Unleash Social Media to Tell Your School's Story ...119
16 Doing What's "Best" for Kids? 127
17 Professional Development—Like a PIRATE! 133

Section III: Coach Like a PIRATE 139

18 ANCHOR Conversations 141
19 The Power of Words 175

SECTION IV: Be a Better Captain 183

20 Go for Greatness 185
21 Dealing with Critics 189
22 Discover the Power of a PLN 193
23 Stay True to Your Roots 197
24 Knowing When to Take the Leadership Leap 201
25 Rest . . . Like a PIRATE 207
26 Call to Action 211

Notes 213
More from Dave Burgess Consulting, Inc. 215
About the Authors 227

Foreword

As I have crisscrossed the globe presenting the *Teach Like a PIRATE* program, one thing has become abundantly clear: The effectiveness of the people who trim the sails and set the course in schools can have an exponential impact on their system. Although it is true that a captain is nothing without a crew, the strength of the person holding the compass and gripping the wheel can make or break the success of the journey.

The problem is, when compared to books centered on teaching and learning, powerful books on leading are in short supply. The *EduPIRATE* movement has been gratifying to be a part of, but I have lost track of how many times I have been asked, "When are you going to publish a PIRATE book for educational leaders?" After years of development and planning, months of writing and rewriting, and many intense moments of deep personal reflection by all parties involved, I can finally answer that question.

Now.

This book is a paradigm-shifting, culture-reshaping, life-transforming manifesto of the highest order. It will change you. More importantly, implementing the treasure within will change your system and allow you to create schools that have both staff and students knocking down the doors to get in.

Much of the real power of the book comes from how Shelley and Beth, both incredible leaders in their own right, have melded their individual experiences, unique strengths and talents, and personal insights into a unified, synergistic masterpiece of extraordinary clarity. You will walk away from the experience of reading this book inspired, motivated to take action, and fully prepared with the ideas, skills, and the mindset necessary to make the amazing an everyday reality on your campus.

Do you remember the passion and enthusiasm you felt when you entered this profession? Remember that *aha!* moment you had when you realized that learning and fun could go hand in hand? Remember how your entire day could be made just by seeing that light-bulb moment of understanding on a child's face? Remember how fulfilling it was to creatively design and then courageously implement powerful learning experiences in your class?

As a PIRATE leader, all of that can still be yours. And now you can create a culture where the best parts of education are the norm for your entire crew and the students you serve. This book is the compass to take you there. Enjoy the voyage!

—Dave Burgess
author of *Teach Like a PIRATE*

The Story of Us

How We Became PIRATE Captains

Beth

Amid the high-stakes testing focus of the No Child Left Behind era, I lost my joy for our great profession. It was the summer of 2014, and I was worn out and ready for a change. At the time, I was too ashamed to admit this fact to my family and friends. After all, I was the professional-development junkie who could never get enough of learning. I loved kids and felt called to education—first as a teacher and later as a principal. My greatest fear in regard to making a career change was failing everyone— my family, friends, and most of all, the students.

With that weariness and fear in mind, I reluctantly agreed to accompany a good friend and colleague to the National Association of Elementary School Principals' conference in Nashville. I figured that, if all else failed, at least we would have fun. On the car ride to the event, my friend provided a listening ear and moral support as I shared my fears and frustrations about education.

At the conference, my friend and I met with other leaders from around the world who were dealing with challenges similar to those I had encountered. One in particular, Jay Billy, asked me if I was on Twitter. I told him I was on Twitter as a faceless egghead and that I didn't really understand the purpose or practicality of yet another form of social media. He then showed me how he used Twitter to connect with the leading experts in our field of education, offer and receive support, and participate in 24/7 professional development. Right then and there, it dawned on me that this kind of support and connection were key elements missing from my life. Yes, I had great family and friends, and my colleagues were wonderful. But after moving into the role of principal, things had gotten lonely; no one else in the building had the same responsibilities as

I did each day. The idea that an app on my phone could immediately put me in touch with hundreds of thousands of other principals who were ready and willing to help me . . . Wow!

Later that same night, Jay asked my friend and me if we had ever heard of the book *Teach Like a PIRATE* by Dave Burgess. After telling us it was one of his favorite books and that Dave presented some of the best professional development sessions he had ever attended, he invited us to a Skype session that Dave was doing in the exhibit hall the next day. Although the book's title sounded familiar, I hadn't read it, nor did I know much about the author. Honestly, because it's so easy to feel inundated by all the professional developmental materials/books/sessions available to (pushed at) us these days, I'm skeptical about "must-read" books or "must-go" conferences. So I didn't commit to attend the workshop, but I did do a little research when I got back to my hotel room that night.

The very first blog post I found was "Lead Like a PIRATE" by Dave's wife, Shelley. I was completely hooked by her passion for her work. That, I realized, was another key element that was missing from my career, and its absence had me wondering if I should leave education. I had let the mundane tasks of leadership overcome the passion and purpose that first drew me into education. When I was in the classroom, I was a complete and wholehearted PIRATE teacher. I pushed the status quo; I analyzed each lesson and always worked to take engagement to new heights to help students learn at higher levels. But when I moved to the role of principal, I fell into the "that's the way it's always been done" mentality. Shelley's blog post had me thinking: Why couldn't I bring this passion from the classroom to leadership? Why couldn't I be me? I immediately purchased Dave's book and began reading. Through the pages of *Teach Like a PIRATE*, I saw the parallels between teaching and my role as a principal.

With my newfound understanding of Twitter, I started following Dave and Shelley and connected to the #tlap community of passionate and dedicated professionals who enthusiastically work to engage students and make school amazing. That hashtag truly changed my life. The #tlap community and the positivity of the group helped me recalibrate my outlook and way of thinking. Within the #tlap community, I connected with other like-minded leaders who offered encouragement and practical support. And when the school year started, I knew I was a PIRATE leader and that I was exactly where I was meant to be.

Shelley

I stepped into my principalship in 2003. I was thirty-one years old, six months pregnant with my second child, and moving from a seventh–twelfth grade school district into a Pre-K–sixth-grade system. I had worked in my previous district my entire career. There, I had built strong relationships, earned credibility and a good reputation. Suddenly, I was walking into a district and school where I didn't know anyone and no one really knew anything about me and what I might offer.

We were in the early stages of the No Child Left Behind era. About 90 percent of our 750 students were Hispanic/Latino, 65 percent of them were classified as English learners, and more than 80 percent of our students were considered "socioeconomically disadvantaged" and qualified for free and reduced lunch. We were the lowest-performing school in the district. By the time students were leaving our school in sixth grade, fewer than 20 percent of them were classified as proficient in their reading, writing, and math skills.

In addition, my new district had just undergone some major reorganization. We were moving out of a multi-track, year-round district to a single-track system. Budgets had been cut along with many positions, including the assistant principal at my new school, had just been eliminated. There was a major rift going on between a group of parents and some of our staff, and when I asked what the biggest challenges were at the school during our very first pre-school staff meeting, gossiping, backstabbing, and staff morale were listed as the top three. Students, families, and staff members were all looking to jump ship. And not everyone was happy that I was coming on board. In fact, in one of the very first conversations I had with a teacher at my new school, who had also been on the interview committee, she told me that she did not support hiring me because she believed we needed a "strong Latino man to whip the school into shape." I told her I hoped to prove her wrong.

While I definitely wasn't referring to it as PIRATE leadership at the time, I was committed to transforming our school. I wanted it to be great. I wanted our students to learn, grow, and thrive. I wanted our staff to be proud of their school and happy to come to work each day. I wanted parents to look no further than right down the street for a safe, loving, academically rich school, so I set my sights on doing just that. Our test scores improved significantly during the course of my tenure as principal, but it wasn't because we were committed to raising test scores. We were committed to working together to create amazing learning experiences for our students. As a leader, I was committed to supporting my staff members in their efforts. While other schools in situations similar to ours were doubling down on test-prep packets, we were adding programs like art, science labs, a Mariachi band, and a summer-school enrichment program where teachers chose what they wanted to teach and students signed up for the experiences that appealed to them.

While other schools were slashing professional-development budgets, we made professional learning and collaboration a top priority and did things like using our funds to buy each grade-level team ninety minutes of collaboration time each week.

While I'll be the first to admit we were far from perfect, we were definitely transforming the culture of our school and turning it into a place where students, families, and staff wanted to be. And when a retiring teacher shared with me that she believed she had the opportunity to be her most creative during her years working for me, I knew we were doing something right.

After five years in the principal role, I moved into central-office leadership as the Director of Student Achievement and ultimately as the Assistant Superintendent of Educational Leadership where I had an amazing opportunity to take the PIRATE spirit with me and work with a great team of people to support all of the schools in our system.

Introduction

A seismic shift seems to occur when moving from the classroom into a position of educational leadership. People look at you differently. They treat you differently. They think you have sold out. They no longer see you as an educator, but as a paper-pushing "administrator." They believe you have crossed over to the dark side and have become one of "them" instead of one of "us," and oftentimes they see you as no longer having the ability to make a life-changing impact on the lives of kids.

Being the person who steers the ship certainly has its challenges, especially when the seas get rough, but we have found that taking the leap from crew member to captain has been an adventurous, invigorating, and worthwhile journey that has led us to discover countless treasures—because we lead like PIRATES!

So what does that mean? Do we really want to lead like pirates? Aren't pirate captains bloodthirsty marauders who stop at nothing to pillage and plunder? Do we really want to turn out like the famous pirate Blackbeard and end up beheaded by the Royal Navy? Of course not. In fact, we want to avoid beheadings (literally and figuratively) at all costs. But notice the similarities between pirate captains and PIRATE leaders: Like Blackbeard, Black Bart, and other pirate captains, PIRATE leaders are courageous. They inspire and influence others to follow them, even in the face of great risk. They lead their crew on a journey to seek great riches and rewards, but the treasure PIRATE leaders seek isn't gold; it is better!

The treasure PIRATE leaders seek is the creation of schools and districts where students and staff are knocking down the doors to get in rather than out. They relentlessly search for ways to make school an amazing place for students, staff members, parents, and communities. These leaders don't simply believe schools can be better; they KNOW schools can be better—even amazing. And we believe *you* have the makings of a PIRATE leader.

PIRATE leadership is about being the kind of leaders we always wanted to be and creating the kinds of schools we dream of for kids. It's about charting a course and setting sail on this incredible journey of educating our future! It's about staying calm when we hit rough seas and letting that passion we have for learning navigate us through—even when some suggest turning back. PIRATE leaders are daring and adventurous, and they are willing to sail into uncharted waters with no guarantee of success, because they know there is a strong possibility of finding treasure of incalculable value.

PIRATE leaders know they have it within them to help make miracles happen for kids, so they work to create the kinds of schools where teachers are encouraged and supported to design the amazing learning experiences kids deserve—experiences that are both rich in content and wildly engaging. They are intentional about transforming schools into extraordinary places where students and staff are willing to go the extra mile because they feel safe, valued, and supported by leaders who believe in their capability to create magic in the classroom. Because of that belief, PIRATE leaders value and tap into the unique talents and gifts of every crew member; they collaborate and aren't afraid to have others take the helm. PIRATE leaders embrace the notion that their primary role is culture first, culture next, culture always.

So what does it take to be a PIRATE leader? It takes a whole lot of **passion**. It takes commitment to **immersing** yourself in the most impactful work. It takes a dedication to building **rapport** that supports an environment where teachers know they are trusted. It takes a strong ability to **ask** good questions and **analyze** what's going on around you. It takes a desire for **transformation** and the courage to implement change.

And it takes daily **enthusiasm**, even on the days when you have to fake it!

This book is a compilation of dynamic strategies to inspire staff, dramatically transform school culture, and build schools where students and staff are running to get in rather than out. We will demonstrate how to take the revolutionary ideas from *Teach Like a PIRATE* and supercharge them for educational leaders. Our goal is to inspire courage and provide practical ideas to help you become the kind of leader you've always hoped you could be. In an era of standardized testing with high-stakes consequences, it can be easy to lose focus on what is really important in our roles as leaders: raising human potential in our students, in our staff, in our parents, and in ourselves.

The biggest inspiration for this book comes from the belief that educators must not lose their motivation, inspiration, and passion when they move into a leadership position. Many leaders feel as though when they move from the classroom to the principalship or other leadership position, they have to become ultra-serious and never show their fun side. Your business card may change, but that doesn't mean you change who you are. Never lose sight of who you are and what made you decide to become an educator. If you are worried because you are more reserved or on the shy side, never fear! Pirates lead in many ways. Some lead with quiet strength; others wear fancy plumes and encourage their crew with shouts of praise. You will have your own unique PIRATE style, one that suits you and serves your crew. But know this: Each risk you take will lead to being more comfortable in your "un-comfort" zone!

Each of us works in a different geographic area and district with varied resources, but one thing doesn't change—we have the opportunity to make a significant difference in the lives of our students through the work we do as leaders and the work we help our staff do. We must inspire questioning, risk taking, creativity, and innovation. We must lead the charge against the sit-and-get mentality and empower our staff and students to be creators instead of consumers. The time is now. We do it for our staff. We do it for our parents. We do it for our kids. We do it for our future. We do it to make a difference.

Surveying the Lay of the Land

Lead Like a PIRATE is set up in four sections with leadership challenges throughout to help you reflect and take action.

Part I: Lead Like a PIRATE

Passion—This chapter explains how to identify passion in yourself, in your staff, and in your students.

Immersion—In this chapter, you'll discover how you can move from merely being present in your school to being truly immersed so you can have the best possible impact on those you lead.

Rapport—Trust is crucial when captaining the ship. This chapter dives into trust-building strategies that will empower you to build rapport with the entire crew.

Ask and Analyze—Great leaders ask great questions and engage in meaningful conversations that empower people to take risks. This chapter focuses on finding the right questions and really listening to and understanding the answers.

Transformation—In this chapter, we will explore ways that leaders transform the mundane into the spectacular. We will examine ways to make essentials, like staff meetings and professional development training, engaging and effective.

Enthusiasm—Enthusiasm and positivity are keys to creating an environment where your teachers and your students are excited about coming to school each day. This chapter offers insights on how to inject enthusiasm into every aspect of leadership so that you—your teachers, students, and surrounding community—get excited about the journey of learning.

Part II: X Marks the Spot: Leadership Treasure

In this section, you will uncover powerful strategies to help build leadership capacity in your organization, regardless of your specific title.

Part III: Coach Like a PIRATE: ANCHOR Conversations

In this section, you'll learn about a coaching model that will help you offer and encourage feedback. You'll discover how to give valuable feedback in a way that instills trust in your crew members and moves everyone forward.

Part IV: Building a Better Captain

Our final section is all about you! Here we'll offer tips and strategies to help you become the best PIRATE leader on and off the ship!

Section I

Lead Like a Pirate

Leading your crew to new, exciting places requires courage. In this section, we'll explore the characteristics you need as a leader in education. At the opening of each chapter, we'll offer insights on how each character trait of a PIRATE leader can help you navigate the seas (C's) of change. We'll also point out the potential dangers to steer clear of.

We're thrilled that you've decided to embark upon this lifelong voyage of excellence with us. Let's set sail!

Navigating the C's of Change

Passion

Compass to Guide You

Commitment:

Understanding and being completely
and totally *into* the mission.

Cannonballs to Avoid

Compliance:

Doing what you are told or following along
without deep understanding.

PASSION

*Working hard for something we don't care about is called stress;
working hard for something we love is called passion.*
—Simon Sinek

*A great leader's courage to fulfill his vision comes from passion,
not position.*
—John Maxwell, *The 21 Irrefutable Laws of Leadership*

*If there is no passion in your life, then have you really lived?
Find your passion, whatever it may be. Become it, and let it
become you and you will find great things happen for you, to
you, and because of you.*
—T. Alan Armstrong

Never underestimate the power of PASSION.
—Eve Sawyer, *The Autobiography of Mick Haines*

We love walking into schools where passion is evident. Positive, inquisitive energy radiates within the walls and around the campus. Everyone wants to be there. Students and educators alike are excited to learn and grow together.

It takes a passionate leader to create this kind of high-energy environment. Thankfully, passion is contagious. Everyone wins when highly effective leaders bring their passion to work because these leaders have a knack for helping those around them uncover their passions and capitalize on them.

> *Everyone wins when highly effective leaders bring their passion to work.*

As a leader, you have an amazing opportunity to make your passion come alive in your school and district. You can use your passions to inspire, transform, and create classrooms and schools that come alive with electric and engaging learning. But if you want your passions to guide and infuse your work, you must first understand what your passions really are—and what they are not. Because let's be honest: You can't be passionate about everything. If you feel the pull of guilt because you don't get excited about every aspect of your work, you aren't alone. Listen, it's okay not to feel overwhelmed with excitement about some things—even if other leaders you know are passionate about those things. What is important is that you know what you are passionate about—and how you can bring that enthusiasm and excitement into your work for the benefit of your students and staff.

Do you know what you are passionate about? Take a few minutes to think about what excites you in terms of content, your professional life, and your personal life.

Content Passion

For teachers, content passion is (or should be!) the subject area they teach. History teachers love learning and talking about history. Math teachers geek out over equations. Food-science teachers get excited about food. (We especially love it when they share their passion by having their classes leave baked goodies in the teacher's lounge.)

As education leaders, our content passion is *leadership*—supporting and guiding our staff and students to success in their teaching and learning endeavors. To us, leadership matters. It matters a lot! We are students of leadership. We read everything we can get our hands on—books by great educational leaders and books from leaders in other fields as well. We know who we are as leaders, what drives us, and what we are passionate about; these passions fuel the work we do. Our passions serve as our compass, guiding us to chart our course.

Below are a few passions we (Beth and Shelley) share when it comes to leadership in education.

- **We are relentless about developing, maintaining, and sustaining positive cultures within our organizations.** *Culture first, culture next, culture always* is a mantra we share and promote.

- **We are passionate about instilling the belief that every educator has the power and the ability to help students—even the students whom others may have written off—accomplish amazing things!** We believe we all have an amazing capacity to have an incredible influence on the lives of children.

- **We are passionate about developing a sense of collective efficacy.** We want to make a difference—not excuses.

- **We are passionate about the belief that it isn't programs that teach kids—it's teachers.** We must empower our teachers to take whatever tools they are given and the tools they have within themselves to make each day extraordinary for their students. An *outstanding* teacher who has nothing but crayons, a chalkboard, and blank pieces of paper in the classroom wins hands down, any day of the week, over the best "program."

- **We are passionate about collaboration.** We are stronger and better collectively than we are individually; we need to hear one another's voices and push one another to learn, to take risks, and to be even better than we thought possible.

- **We are passionate about using the influence we have as leaders to inspire other leaders, adult learners, and teachers to do incredible work.** As a result, we are passionate about great coaching and engaging in rich dialogue around teaching and learning that ultimately has a powerful impact on student learning.

Specific to leadership, what are you most passionate about?

Professional Passion

Think about all things you love about this crazy, wild, wonderful business of being an educator. Those are your professional passions. They are the passions that drew you to education in the first place. And they are the reasons that compel you to continue to grow and serve as a leader.

I (Beth) am what Dave Burgess refers to in *Teach Like a PIRATE* as an educational freak. I get passionate about so many things related to this great profession. I love all the subject and content areas. I love professional development. I am also particularly passionate about effective utilization of technology, developing innovative practices in our schools to ensure high levels of learning for all, and personalizing learning for students and staff. In short, I love it all so much, in fact, that I have to work on not overwhelming people with my enthusiasm and energy for learning.

I (Shelley) am passionate about making a difference in the lives of students. I believe that a quality education is the great equalizer, and I am passionate about making sure every child receives an amazing education every minute of every day they are in school. I am passionate about eliminating the "achievement gap." I believe every child, regardless of their socioeconomic and cultural background, has the desire to learn and to be exceptional. I believe we (all educators and school leaders) have the knowledge, the expertise, the capacity, and the responsibility to help our students realize they are exceptional. I am passionate about providing every child with rich learning opportunities that prepare them to thrive in any subject area. I believe we have the power, the ability, and the obligation to make sure every child leaves our classrooms and schools fully prepared to excel in the next phase of their educational experience. I am passionate about making sure all children think of themselves as smart, and I am passionate about seeing things in children that they don't yet see in themselves and about nurturing and encouraging them to share their gifts and their talents with the world.

Within the profession of education, but not specific to leadership, what are you passionate about?

Personal Passion

Personal passions are those things outside of your profession that excite and energize you. They are the things you can talk about for hours, and they are what you invest your time, money, and energy in—because you *love* them.

Outside of education, I (Beth) am completely passionate about my family. I love traveling with them, exploring the family farm, and attending my children's sporting events. I love to read, travel, and try new restaurants, and I enjoy spending time with friends. I love St. Louis Cardinals baseball and Mizzou Tiger football.

Outside of education, I (Shelley) am also extremely passionate about my family, so much so that I ultimately changed the course of my career to be home more with my children and to grow a business with my husband. I'm passionate about travel and family vacations; I love to explore new places, new cultures, and new food. While not an artist myself, I love art and compelling photographs. I love to read, I love to be with friends, and I love to get caught up in engaging conversations with people who push and challenge my thinking.

Outside of your profession, what are you most passionate about?

What We're *Not* Passionate About

We will be the first to admit that we are not passionate about everything we do in our roles as school leaders. And that's okay. We don't have to love *every* minute of *every* day or every task on our to-do lists. Neither do you! Below is a list of just a few things we are *not* passionate about.

Although some of these items may be necessary or even beneficial, they are not what cause us to wake up in the morning with a fist-pumping *Yes! I-can't-wait-to-go-to-work-today* mentality. A few things we are not passionate about:

- meetings for the sake of meeting
- uniform and dress-code policies and violations
- student discipline
- disaster drills
- writing fifty-page site/district plans
- compliance issues
- state tests
- sports supervision

While we all have things about our work that we don't love to do, what we are passionate about is handing those things in the most effective and efficient way possible. They need to be handled, and handled well, but we are passionate about finding ways to ensure our days are not consumed with them.

Why Knowing Your Passions Matters

So why do we think it is so important to share our passions with you? To share them with our teams? Our communities? Our passions are what drive us! They help us determine the direction we point our compass. They influence the plans we put in place, the decisions we make, the actions we take, and the reactions we have. We want our crew to know us, to know who we are, what we believe in, what we stand for. We don't want them to have to guess. We don't want them to ever feel blindsided. So we share our passions with our crew freely and openly. We believe it's a critical part of being transparent and authentic as a leader.

Taking time to identify your passions as a leader has a twofold benefit. First, in the moments that are particularly tough, or when you are dealing with issues that you are not passionate about, you can draw energy to press forward from a content, professional, or personal passion. For example, I (Beth) dread typing up observation evaluations because of the paperwork involved. But my passion for supporting teachers and bringing technology and innovation into the classrooms brings relevance to the tedium of that paperwork.

Secondly, being in tune with and vocal about your passions can help those around you to better understand you. Additionally, your self-awareness may help you avoid feelings of frustration and conflict that can easily arise when others don't really understand what's most important to you or what makes you "tick."

So don't be afraid to put yourself out there. Share who you are, what you're passionate about, and how it motivates you to lead.

Why Knowing Your Crew's Passions Matters

Another leadership component that sets PIRATE leaders apart is our role in helping others identify and tap into *their* passions. One of the early mistakes I (Shelley) made as a leader was believing that everyone would be as enthusiastic as I about the things I was passionate about in education. I actually believed that when I got excited about a new and better way of doing something and shared it with my staff, they all would be equally excited about it. I just knew they would be willing to make the change the next day! If you have been in a leadership role longer than about two months, you can imagine how well that went over. Over time, I discovered that *passionate* leaders also need *patience* if we want to initiate positive change in our schools and districts that lasts. Once we light a spark, we need to give it time to catch. We need to nurture it, feed it, stoke it, give it proper attention, and let it develop into a slow and steady burn that ultimately engulfs our school or district community. Likewise, we need to be passionate about stoking the flames of others. We need to encourage and support the members of our crew, empowering them to explore their own passions and then to find ways to use them to become better educators and help the school or district become a better place.

In her book *The Multiplier Effect: Tapping the Genius Inside Our Schools*, Liz Wiseman and her co-authors say this about the importance of helping your crew members discover and unleash their passions:

There are leaders who use their intelligence to amplify the smarts and capabilities of the people around them. When these leaders walk into a room, light bulbs go on over people's heads; ideas flow and problems get solved. People get smarter in their presence because they are given permission to think. These are the leaders who inspire employees to stretch themselves to deliver results that surpass expectations. These leaders tend to make everyone around them better and more capable. These leaders are like Multipliers—intelligence Multipliers.

'Top Three' Activity

One fun, low-risk activity we do in our workshops to help jump-start the conversation about passion is called "Top Three," and it's great to do with your staff. First, ask your staff members to identify their top three favorite movies of all time. (You could replace movies with another topic if you want.) This should be done quickly and without collaborating with others. After about two minutes, share your top three favorite movies with your staff and then explain that movies can tell a lot about a person and that you can find a common theme between these movies.

For example, my (Beth's) current top three favorite movies (which change often, by the way) are *The Goonies, Bridesmaids,* and *The Wizard of Oz.* The common theme of these movies is that no matter the circumstances, the underdog can always rise above and be successful. That theme is a strong parallel to my personal life. My parents were fifteen when I was born, which meant I had to overcome difficult social and economic challenges during a time when the odds were not in my favor. Through relationships, role models, resources and resiliency, I knew I wanted to make a difference for other people in their lives. Today, I openly share my story with my staff, in part because I tend to take it personally when someone thinks, for whatever reason, that a child with a challenging home life can't succeed at high levels.

My (Shelley's) top three movies are *The Breakfast Club, Pretty Woman,* and *Titanic.* They share the common theme of having central characters who are judged or stereotyped based on surface-level attributes. People make judgments about who these characters are because of their place in society, the amount of money they have, the clothes they wear, the group they belong to etc., but as their stories progress, it's clear that each of these characters is so much more than what they were given credit for in the beginning. Each one has something special and unique about them, and when you take the time to get to know them, you discover amazing things about who they truly are. As an educator, I have always worked in districts and schools that others might describe as having demographics that are "challenging" and where students, families, and entire communities were dismissed because of the color of their skin, the language they spoke, or the money they didn't have. My passion is discovering the untapped talents in students, parents, and staff members so their incredible gifts don't go unnoticed or unused.

After we share our three movies and the common theme, we ask the participants to find the theme in the three movies they wrote down and to share with a partner what their top three movies reveal about their passion as an educator. You might also have your staff members post their top three movies and corresponding passion in the staff lounge for others to see.

Another thought/idea is to create a "passion wall" for staff with a picture and statement about something they are passionate about. Teachers could do something similar with students in their classrooms. The point is to get to know what drives the people around you. And if you're a leader, the point is to help them tap into those passions and use them to make school amazing.

There are many ways you can share your passions with your school team. For example, we tap into our passions for technology and social-media and share through our blogs as well as through daily social media posts. We also push ourselves to try new things that may be better than past practices—like morphing a standard newsletter into a part-text, part-video digital communication, or participating in online read-alouds that demonstrate the importance of literacy while creating opportunities to connect digitally with families at home.

Becoming a PIRATE leader is a journey. We encourage you to use your passions to help you chart your course and to help you recalculate when you get off course. We also recommend keeping a captain's log in the form of notes, a journal, lists, or even a blog. Keep track of some of the day's highlights and challenges, take time to reflect, and as you move forward on the journey, take time to look back so you can continually measure your growth as a leader. Mistakes will happen. As long as you learn from them, you keep the ship on course toward the goal of finding educational treasure.

Passion Challenge

- Take some time to think about your passions. Write them down.

- Reflect. Does your staff know what you're passionate about and what you stand for? Create a "What do I stand for?" document/video/slideshow/blog, etc. and share it! Looking for ideas? Check out Beth's introductory slideshow here: bit.ly/houfintro.

- Do you know what each member of your staff is passionate about? If not, how might you encourage your staff to bring more of what they are passionate about with them to work each day?

- Do your parents and students know what you are passionate about? How might they get to know you better?

- How might you get to know the passions of your students and families?

- Does your supervisor know your passions and what you stand for in education? Do you know the passions of those who lead you? How might you facilitate this?

 Share your thoughts, ideas, and artifacts with the *Lead Like a PIRATE* community using the #LeadLAP hashtag.

Immersion

Compass to Guide You

Credible:

Has a deep understanding and continues to grow in depth. Walks the walk!

Cannonballs to Avoid

Counterfeit:

Gives the appearance understanding and believing but is easily turned. Talks the talk but fails to walk the walk.

observe instruction and provide teachers with feedback. That realization was the catalyst for me to start prioritizing my time and to make better use of my team so I could immerse myself in what mattered most.

Dive In!

It's easy to get focused on the urgent tasks to the neglect of important, long-term goals. But the reality is, if you want to transform what is happening in your school or district, you have to immerse yourself in the work that has the highest impact on increasing student learning and building a rich, powerful, and positive culture. It isn't reasonable to expect that spending only 20 percent of your time doing highly impactful work will yield the type of results you want. You need systems and strategies that give you the freedom to spend the highest percentage of your time doing the most impactful work. As leaders, we can show up to work each day with nothing on our to-do list and still be busy all day simply reacting to what's thrown at us from the moment we walk in the door. We can be exhausted at the end of the day and hope that what we did that day helped our school to change, but hope on its own doesn't create change. Action does. Intentional time and focus devoted to the right things are what will ultimately propel you forward.

Hope on its own doesn't create change.
Action does.

But it is not enough to be present; we have to be truly immersed in the work, not just the job. In *Teach Like a PIRATE*, Dave uses the analogy of the lifeguard and the swimmer to describe different types of teachers in the classroom. The analogy works for leaders too. If you are a lifeguard leader, you are present, but you are sitting up in your tower observing. Yes, you are trying to keep people on track, keep them safe, and keep them doing what they are supposed to be doing, but you mostly work through observation, blowing your whistle and pointing out when people are breaking the rules. Leaders who are swimmers come down off their towers and get in the pool with their teams—especially when they are in the deep end. Unafraid of getting wet, they are immersed in the work of teaching, learning, and culture building—the good, the bad, and the ugly of it all.

Immersed leaders create environments where people feel safe taking risks.

For leaders, the goal is to be invited into real conversations about the teaching and learning happening on campus right now—not just the conversations that are designed for show. How can we contribute to making things better if true struggles and challenges are hidden from us? Immersed leaders create environments where people feel safe taking risks and know they won't be criticized for making a mistake. If you are an immersed leader, people won't try to hide their weaknesses from you; rather, they will seek you out as someone who can help them learn and grow.

One of my (Shelley's) proudest moments as a principal came while working with one of my grade-level teams. They were reviewing data they had just received from a writing assessment where students had been asked to read a passage and summarize it. The data wasn't good; the majority of the students had not scored well. Rather than beat them up about it, I asked the team a question about what they thought the challenge was. After a long pause, one of the teachers said, "Honestly, I don't really know how to teach kids to write good summaries." Her colleagues nodded in agreement, and I had just been invited into the real conversation! I thanked her for taking a risk and sharing that with me, and then I offered to help. I let the team know that teaching summaries was actually something I was good at. We proceeded to work together to plan a series of lessons to teach students how to write good summaries. I taught the lessons to one class, and the team was able to observe me. We spent time debriefing and, ultimately, they took over teaching lessons with me able to observe and provide them with support. The end result was that our students got continuously better at writing their summaries!

Highly effective leaders—PIRATE leaders—roll up their sleeves and participate in the work alongside their staff and community members. That personal involvement means they always know the "pulse" of their school or district. They invest time in both the big and small moments of leadership. They regularly immerse themselves in classroom observations and engage with teachers and teams about how to ensure student learning thrives. And they can often be found on the playground jumping rope with a group of students, or in the cafeteria chatting with kids at the table, or reading a book to a room full of kindergarteners, or talking with a parent volunteer in the hallway. No matter where these leaders are, they practice being fully present and intentional with their time and energy.

The same is true when it comes to learning and professional growth. Immersed leaders constantly read books, articles, blog posts, and other literature in an effort to stay current on effective practices and ideas. On professional-development days, it is easy to see which leaders are merely present and which are immersed in their desire to improve. A present leader will be off to the side, reading the paper or working on a task unrelated to the learning. Much like the lifeguard, this leader watches from the perch. In contrast, truly immersed leaders will be at the table with their team, soaking up and contributing to the learning. Whether it's learning, connecting, or setting the course for their schools, immersed leaders can always be found side by side with their staff and school communities.

Finding Time to L.E.A.D.

I must govern the clock, not be governed by it.
—Golda Meir

All good leaders want to be immersed, but the big question is *how?* A school leader's job can feel intimidating and overwhelming at times. It can seem as if the job never ends. If you are a principal or administrator, you probably feel as if your days are already jam-packed; adding anything else seems unrealistic.

We hear you. We know you're busy. But we also know that with the right systems, strategies, and focus, it is possible for you to make the kind of impact you desire. The following activity is one we have done with numerous leadership teams to help them analyze their daily schedules and begin to make small changes that can have *big* impact. You can do this on your own or with your leadership team.

For this activity, you'll need sticky notes in three different sizes: large, regular, and small. Write down the tasks you do as a leader in a typical week (we know that there are many weeks that aren't actually "typical," but you get the idea). Next, review the list and decide which of those tasks you do that have a *high* impact on student learning and building a positive culture—those things that make the biggest difference. Write these items on your large sticky notes and position them at the top of the surface you are working on. Next, write down the weekly tasks you do that have medium impact on student learning and culture on the medium-sized sticky notes. Put these under your large sticky notes. Finally, write down weekly or daily tasks you do that have minimal or no impact on student learning and culture on the small sticky notes and place these below your medium sticky notes. Check your calendar and compare your schedule with the sticky notes to be sure you haven't left anything out of the three categories. You should now have a pyramid of sorts, organized from the most impactful work you do as a leader to the least impactful work you do.

We have to be intentional about taking control of our daily schedules and prioritizing the most powerful work.

The second part of this activity is to now reorient the sticky notes based on how you actually spend your time each week. Move the tasks that you spend the most time on to the top of your pyramid and put the activities you spend the least amount of time on at the bottom. Many times in our workshops, we have experienced leaders just flipping their pages upside down because they feel they spend most of their time on the tasks that have the smallest impact on student learning and culture. This is a powerful, paradigm-shifting moment of self-reflection for Lead Like a PIRATE participants, as they realize they spend most of their time doing the work that has the least amount of influence on student learning. As leaders, we all have to be intentional about taking control of our daily schedules and prioritizing the most powerful work. If we aren't spending the majority of our time doing the work that is most impactful, we will never get the type of transformation we are hoping for in our schools or districts.

So how do you reorganize your time? How can you make time for what matters most? You have to L.E.A.D.:

Leverage Systems

Elevate the Impact

Activate a Team

Delete, Delete, Delete!

Leverage Systems

Some tasks can take up an inordinate amount of time (and cause stress as a result) simply because you don't have a system in place to help you handle it. Oftentimes, if you can strengthen a system or create a new one, you can recapture some valuable time. As an example, when I (Shelley) first started as a principal, I was the only administrator on campus with more than 750 students. I honestly spent hours handling student discipline. Students were in the office all the time for one minor infraction after another. I can't count the number of times I was called by the office staff to come back and handle the students who had been sent to the office for disciplinary reasons, most of which were pretty minor. I took this challenge to my staff and painted a picture of what was happening in the front office. I then asked them to help me create a system to efficiently and effectively handle student discipline issues. The first step toward developing a system is to better understand the problems, so we worked together to generate a list of the issues from the teacher perspective, office staff perspective, and my perspective as the principal. Below is a list of the primary concerns from each perspective:

1. Sometimes teachers get frustrated with a student and they need some space.

2. The office staff shouldn't be responsible for supervising kids on a regular basis.

3. The principal needs protected time to be in classrooms, at team meetings, etc. and can't respond immediately to minor discipline concerns.

From there, we worked collectively to create a system to address those three core concerns. While the system we designed then may not be the same system we would design today, it worked for our school at the time. It was actually a strengthened version of a system the school had used in the past called "discipline partners." In essence, when a minor discipline issue arose, the teacher could send the child to the partner classroom with some work to do for a little bit (which helped address the teacher's concern). It the teacher felt the infraction warranted a conversation with the principal, they could send to the office a referral rather than the child (which helped address the office staff's concern). If I had a referral, I committed to making sure I met with the student to discuss the issue within twenty-four hours, but it wouldn't necessarily be right away (which addressed my concern as the principal).

Within a matter of days of implementing this new system, I was able to reallocate several hours of my time away from minor discipline issues to areas that had bigger impact on student learning and culture.

Elevate the Impact

Elevating the impact is all about rethinking tasks that seem to have little impact on student learning and figuring out how to use time more wisely. Bus duty, hall duty, and lunch duty are all tasks that typically fall on the small sticky notes, and they may belong there if they are simply about supervision and monitoring. But these are actually the best times of my (Beth's) day because I am determined to elevate their impact and do more than just monitor for safety infractions. I use the time to triage for potential problems. I use it to put smiles on the faces of our students by putting on crazy dance parties and giving high fives. I use the time to nurture those important relationships that aren't always as easy to build when you are the principal. I use it to be truly immersed in the lives of my students.

As a PIRATE leader, you can take tasks typically relegated to the smallest sticky notes and find powerful ways to dramatically elevate their impact. When you approach these tasks from the viewpoint of a swimmer, rather than a lifeguard, they can become valuable opportunities to enhance school culture.

Activate a Team

There are many tasks we do as leaders that we don't have to do alone. We can ask for help and *activate a team*. People are less likely to tear down systems they help to build.

> ### People are less likely to tear down systems they help to build.

One task that I (Beth) spent much time on in my early years of principalship was class lists. I took feedback on splits, parent requests, and the knowledge I had about students to create the best class lists possible. It literally took me days to do this. I knew there had to be a better way, so I reached out to my principal friends in other districts and learned that some of them involved teachers in creating these lists. Empowered to make a change in the way I had been working, I sat down with the leadership team and brainstormed how to best use our teachers to make the class lists for our elementary school. We set some guidelines and, just like that, our staff worked together to build amazing classes, looking at the strengths and growth areas of each student (and teacher). What previously took me *days* to accomplish was completed in a matter of hours by the teams.

Teams don't always have to be teacher or staff teams; you can also activate student teams. When I (Shelley) first started as a principal, I learned that several activities had been banned from the playground because of poor behavior of past students and fights that started during the activity. Soccer and football were two of these activities. There was very little for kids to do on our asphalt-and-gravel playground, and the reality was the more activities we took away, the more problems we had during recess and lunch periods. Because our school had multiple recesses and lunch times, I ended up on playground supervision for almost two hours every day in an effort to keep the peace on the playground and avoid having my office full of kids after lunch. We had a few fifth- and sixth-grade boys who were often in the middle of the trouble that brewed on the playground. They were also the ones who desperately wanted to play football and soccer, so I activated a student team charged with designing soccer games and football games for students to play, but they would need to alleviate the concerns the staff had with them in the past. The children eagerly went about their task, creating a set of rules and guidelines for play so these games could be brought back to our playground. The student leaders were empowered to help make sure everyone followed the rules. Ultimately, by adding more things to do on the playground and empowering a student team to help design the new system, I was able to dramatically cut down on the time I spent on playground supervision. The students were more committed to following rules they had helped create, and the problems these activities had caused in the past quickly disappeared.

The students were more committed to following rules they had helped create.

When my (Beth's) school rolled out our 1:1 Chromebook initiative, we found we were inundated with many new tasks. First, our technology work orders quadrupled. Our tech department could not keep up. Another big issue was that our staff was not properly trained on how to effectively use these new tools in the classroom. Instead of dropping the whole idea of 1:1 because of these challenges, we activated a student tech team. We have four Tech Agents that now help with these tasks and so much more. Our Tech Agents:

- clean, maintain, and update our computer lab
- troubleshoot tech issues in the building
- prepare daily announcements in a variety of formats (webpage, email to students and teachers, printed for outside front office, and a slide-show to present on large monitors in cafeteria at breakfast and lunch)
- check student help-desk requests for repairs on student Chromebooks
- meet one day a week with the district's instructional technology facilitator to learn new trends and apps for the teacher toolbox they have created (bit.ly/FMSTechInterns)
- meet one day a week with the district's technology support team for assistance in tech issues

This student-led team has also set up our Twitter feed using our school hashtag #fmsteach. Using Tweetbeam, they make sure the feed runs on the monitor in the entryway of our school. They've also presented digital-citizenship sessions to our students and have initiated a school-wide *upstander* campaign. (An upstander is someone who is the opposite of a bystander. It is a person who either "stands up" to help a person in need or goes to get a person who can help.)

The 2016–2017 school year has truly been an innovation experience with our student Tech Agents. These students have redefined the student tech-intern program at our school. They have reaffirmed my belief that students are our greatest resource. Because they have been empowered to lead, these eighth graders will enter high school next year where there is already a plan in place for them to take their expertise to the next level. This team is also now on the conference circuit, sharing their practices with other schools.

Delete. Delete. Delete.

An important part of finding time to lead has to do with letting go. Sometimes you simply have to lighten your load. I (Beth) used to ask for new staff to turn in lesson plans each week. I spent so much time reading and reviewing these plans, asking questions, and providing feedback. Ultimately, my review took time away from other important things and added several hours to my work week. I realized this review could be easily done during classroom observations; it was obvious within the first few minutes in the classroom whether the teacher's lesson plan needed support. When I deleted weekly lesson-plan reviews from my to-do list, it freed up more time to be in classrooms, which in turn gave me more time to have conversations with staff on the lessons that were being taught.

Sometimes you simply have to lighten your load.

In the assistant superintendent role, I (Shelley) took seriously my responsibility to help support our principals with getting back some of their time. One simple example of deleting a time sucker for them was eliminating many emails from their inbox. A principal could easily be away from the office for a couple of hours only to return to an inbox full of emails. In an attempt to eliminate as many of these emails as possible, I worked with my team to end the practice of sending the large number of emails coming out from our team. We started sending a weekly "Leading the Learning" document which was emailed to principals by early Monday morning. In addition to including resources and information about things we were learning about and focused on as a system, it had all of the announcements, reminders, calendar items, etc. that had been going out in separate emails to principals. Unless something was incredibly time sensitive, we no longer emailed notes throughout the week. We included the information in the Monday document. Principals loved the resource because it saved them time and kept all of the information they needed organized in one place (bit.ly/2msgy30).

IMMERSION CHALLENGE

- Take the Sticky-Note Challenge. Look at your calendar for the next two weeks and evaluate how you are spending your time. If you are not immersed in activities that have high impact, make at least three adjustments to your calendar that get you more time to do the more impactful work.

- L.E.A.D. your way to the elimination of several of your small notes. Choose one or two of those little- to no-impact items and determine whether you can leverage a system, elevate the impact, activate a team, or simply delete!

- Plan ahead. Look at your calendar for the next few months. Schedule high-impact work that often gets pushed to the side (i.e., classroom visits and providing feedback). Do not allow other things to take their place.

 Share your thoughts, ideas, and artifacts with the *Lead Like a PIRATE* community using the #LeadLAP hashtag.

Navigating the C's of Change

Rapport

Compass to Guide You

Compassion:

Has true empathy and understanding.
Regard for everyone.

Community:

Dedicated to the mission of the crew
and doesn't care about credit.

Cannonballs to Avoid

Callousness:

Not caring of other members of your crew.
Decisions made with total disregard for others.

Competition:

Only wants to win and doesn't care about
the mission.

RAPPORT

Over time, I have come to this simple definition of leadership:
Leadership is getting results in a way that inspires trust.
—Stephen M. R. Covey, *The Speed of Trust*

Trust is knowing that when a team member does push you,
they're doing it because they care about the team.
—Patrick Lencioni, *The Five Dysfunctions of a Team*

You're either building trust or destroying it.
—Unknown

If we want meaningful change, we have to make a connection
to the heart before we can make a connection to the mind.
—George Couros, *The Innovator's Mindset*

I
f you have strong teacher unions in your system, you know there are times when contract negotiations can be tense. The longer negotiations take, the more teachers unite by wearing black on a particular day, "working to the rule," and by participating in practices that are intended to show their unity in their cause. We had a time like this during my (Shelley's) principalship. Teachers across our system were

united and organized. At the same time, the teachers at my site and I had been working really well together and implemented several practices we knew were benefiting our students. In the midst of negotiations controversy, our school's first- and second-grade teachers and I had been working on a plan to extend the school day for their students by twenty-five minutes per day so their school day would be equal to the school day of the third- through sixth-grade students. The twenty-five fewer minutes was a district-wide practice, and we wanted to change that practice at our school. Because several of our teachers were also committed to their union and wanted to support its efforts, they had some legitimate concerns about the timing. They didn't want their extension of the day to be seen as lack of support for their union's cause. Ultimately, though, they decided to have a conversation with their union leadership about what they wanted to do. The teachers at our site were in unanimous agreement that they wanted to move forward and, ultimately, the union entered into a side letter of agreement with us and approved us moving forward with the school-day extension. In many systems, coming to an agreement like this during a period of intense negotiations would be unthinkable.

So how does something like this happen in a school or district? The answer is that PIRATE leaders make it a priority to build rapport and relationships. They do this with staff, with parents, with students, with community members, with their colleagues, and with their supervisors. They invest the time in getting to know people and determining their strengths and areas of growth potential. They learn about their crew members' passions, their best hopes, and their worst fears. And they invest this time with everyone—even those whom previous leaders had written off. When they do this well, they can move mountains! PIRATE leaders embrace opportunities to hear multiple perspectives, and they value the contribution each person makes to the organization—and they tell them so. They treat their teams with the dignity and respect they deserve. The payoff is huge.

It Starts with Trust

At the core, good rapport and great relationships are built on trust.

Why is it that one leader can present a new initiative or program to a school and it is received with open arms, while another leader introduces the exact same idea—with the exact same level of passion and enthusiasm—but the program barely gets off the ground?

Why can one administrator be in classrooms on a daily basis, snap photos of teachers and their work, post them on Twitter, and then have engaging conversations about the lesson afterward, while another leader would have a grievance filed against them for doing the same?

Why can one principal join in grade-level or department professional learning communities (PLCs) anytime and be a valued participant, while other leaders are asked to stay out unless invited?

Why is one administrator invited by teachers to watch lessons and provide feedback, while other administrators only get to see the "dog-and-pony-show lessons" the teacher prepared for an evaluation?

How can one principal share unfavorable test data with the community and convince parents to leave their children in their school and in their care, while parents in another school with similar test data see the numbers and immediately head for a different school or district?

The answer is *trust*!

Nothing leaders do matters much without the trust of their teams and communities. It's nearly impossible to build the kind of schools we dream of—the kind where students and staff are beating down the doors to get in rather than out—if we don't have their trust. Trust is the oxygen of our school systems. You can't see it, hear it, touch it, or feel it, but without it, you will find yourself struggling to survive.

> *Nothing leaders do matters much without the trust of their teams and communities.*

When I (Shelley) first moved into the role of Director of Student Achievement, our district had entered into program improvement under No Child Left Behind. We were required to contract with an outside consultant to come in and help us improve our schools across the system. One thing the consultants identified after visiting all 400 classrooms in our district was the need to strengthen some of our pedagogical practices across the system. In partnership with our district's external evaluator, we created a set of instructional practices to be infused in classrooms across the system. The pedagogical practices selected were excellent; they were grounded in research and supported by district-wide data and observations. We spent a significant amount of time, energy, and money on professional learning for principals, teachers, and coaches in order to develop common understanding of the practices and to deepen our understanding of what they looked like in classrooms.

And then, over time, those practices turned into a checklist. Administrators all over our district put them on clipboards and carried the checklists with them into classrooms. Those checklists unintentionally produced an almost instantaneous lack of trust between the teachers and administrators. Instead of improving pedagogical practices, the checklists—and the resulting distrust they fostered—led to hours of contract negotiations and creation of new committees to deal with the "crisis" and the clear "lack of respect" administrators exhibited to teachers. Teachers created "fake lessons" to pull out when administrators walked in the room so they could "earn their check marks and get on with their teaching." Teachers came in force to board meetings to rally around getting rid of this "insane" new protocol.

The ability to have authentic, meaningful conversations about teaching and learning was lost because people were so focused on the checklist and the lack of trust its use implied. It took time for us to work through this as a district, as we had to rebuild trust. The entire experience taught me valuable lessons that I took with me as I moved into the assistant superintendent role and had to make decisions about what to do and what not to do in planning for the initiatives I was charged to lead.

Without trust, we don't truly collaborate; we merely coordinate or, at best, cooperate. It is trust that transforms a group of people into a team.
—Stephen M. R. Covey, *Smart Trust*

Every Move You Make

As a leader, every action you take (or don't take), every interaction you have, every decision you make or leave unmade, every expression on your face, the tone in your voice, or the body language you convey— everything about you—either earns or erodes trust. You can't leave this one to chance! To be a PIRATE leader, you need to have a heightened awareness of what trust is, how you earn it, and how you can lose it.

Trust is instrumental to the success of any organization. So how do you earn that much-needed trust from your staff and school community? Stephen M. R. Covey explains in *The Speed of Trust* that the first step is understanding that trust is made up of two essential components: character and competence.

Character is all about your integrity; competence is about having the knowledge and the skill set to do the work. You can have impeccable character as a leader, but if you don't have an exceptional grasp of pedagogical practices, teachers won't trust you to make good decisions about curriculum or to engage with them in meaningful dialogue about their lessons. And you can be an expert in teaching and learning, but if you don't know how to treat people or don't follow through on promises, people will be suspicious of you and won't commit to the work, even if it's good work.

Earning Trust as a Leader

Earning trust as a leader begins with getting to know people and letting them get to know you. This is a simple yet challenging task. Time is always at a premium, which means it's essential to maximize every opportunity and make every interaction and communication you have with people count! Don't waste a single moment. Rapport and trust building can begin even before the first days of school.

Prior to beginning our leadership positions, we each took time to connect with those with whom we would be working daily. We sent letters home, held back-to-school get-togethers and meet-and-greets. We scheduled one-on-one meetings with every staff member to hear their perspectives and get to know them personally. We made ourselves available for parents, students, and the community to meet with us. We attended school events and extracurricular activities. We took time to share our personal missions, passions, and enthusiasm for our profession, and we asked others to share theirs with us. Our stakeholders got to know our families, our backgrounds, and even our favorite foods, movies, and sports teams. Sometimes leaders are made to believe that they can't show their human side. PIRATE leaders know people don't trust those they can't connect with or relate to in some way.

> *Real progress only comes from true commitment to a shared vision and through a culture built on trust.*

We have known leaders who have made illusory gains and some forward progress in their schools without having the trust of their team, but typically these are leaders who have built a culture of compliance. Any gains made through creating a culture of compliance are short lived. Real progress only comes from true commitment to a shared vision and through a culture built on trust.

Giving Trust as a Leader

When people move into school-leadership roles, the stress of being responsible for the success of students in their school or district becomes palpable. Knowing that, ultimately, the buck stops with them as the leader can create an internal struggle. On the one hand, the goal is to build a climate and culture where people are empowered to make decisions, take risks, and push themselves to continually learn and grow. On the other hand, the leader secretly worries: *What if they make the wrong decisions?* As a result, leaders (particularly new leaders) can easily fall into the trap of feeling as if they have to be the expert on everything and be responsible for every decision. The truth, of course, is that it's impossible for one person to be the expert on everything that happens in a school or district. And we can tell you from experience that if you try to be the chief captain, cook, and bottle washer, you will exhaust yourself and, most likely, still fall short in too many areas. You must be willing to give your trust to the members of your crew.

We know this can be hard. We know you want to do the right thing. We know you feel responsible. We know you are fearful that people will make bad choices, but giving your trust to others is essential for the success of your students, teachers, and entire school community.

When I (Shelley) first became a principal, there was evidence all around me that people weren't trusted in our school. The teacher supply room was locked. The only way to get supplies was to submit a form to the office. One of the people trusted with the keys would fill the orders on Tuesdays and Thursdays. If a teacher had a brilliant idea on Thursday night about something they wanted to do, and needed some simple supplies, they were out of luck. Each teacher had a "copy limit" for the month. They had their own unique code they entered at the copy machine, and when they reached that limit, they could not make more copies. Paper and other supplies were rationed. A new textbook adoption for reading/language arts had just occurred and they had all been told that they weren't to use anything else except that specific program, and they were to use it with fidelity. The list goes on and on. In the one-on-one meetings I set up with staff members when I first started, the number of people who talked about these practices and lack of trust they felt because of them was staggering. The mistrust of the system stifled their creativity. Tired of being told "no," people just stopped asking for the resources and support they needed. One of my first acts as principal was to get rid of all the obstacles I could. I gave them my trust, in many ways, even before I had earned theirs. As a result, they began to trust me.

Two phenomenal resources we recommend if you are interested in reading more about building organizations grounded in trust are *The Speed of Trust: The One Thing That Changes Everything* by Stephen M. R. Covey and *Everybody Matters: The Extraordinary Power of Caring for Your People Like Family* by Bob Chapman. Read them, implement what you learn, and watch what happens as trust grows.

Strategies to Build Rapport

One strategy to begin building trust and rapport with your students, staff, and community members is simply taking time to talk to them and, more importantly, to listen. Relationships aren't built on memos and emails. Take time to let people get to know you and, in turn, be passionately and compassionately interested in them.

While we're discussing the need to connect with the people you serve, we have to touch on technology. You'll read more later in this book about some of the many ways technology, social media, and other digital tools can help simplify communication. Technology, such as mass emails, automatic phone messages, and up-to-date websites, can be efficient and valuable, but never underestimate the power of face-to-face interaction or even simply picking up the phone.

Don't let the need for efficiency override the need to build rapport with your staff and your school community.

Yes! We want you to maximize your time by using the tech tools at your disposal; but we want you use them wisely. Don't let the need for efficiency override the need to build rapport with your staff and your school community. And for goodness' sake, don't allow technology to be a barrier between you and your staff or community. (Voice mail and robocalls may be efficient, but make sure they don't take the place of real communication.)

Being visible and accessible as a leader is an accelerant to building trust. How easy is it for your families, your staff, your students, your community partners to have conversations with you? Is there a deep layer of barricades that keep them from you? Be mindful of the potential unintentional trust busters that may have a negative effect on the relationships you have with your stakeholders.

Use of Technology

With daily advances in technology, there are literally endless possibilities for connecting with stakeholders. Later in this book, you'll learn about a few of the ways we've used various social-media platforms to connect with our school communities and share our school's story. For now though, we'll share just one example of one tool that helps to make communication easy.

I (Beth) was introduced to the newsletter Smore (smore.com) at a principals' conference in 2014. At first, I didn't see how it was better than my traditional newsletter or my blog. The more I looked at it, though, the more I loved the visual nature and user-friendliness. I saw the opportunity it created to make my newsletter more of a two-way communication tool.

One of my early Smore flyers was for our debut "No Worksheet Holiday." I posted the link to the flyer on our Facebook page, Twitter, and sent it out in the

Smore Samples

No Worksheet Holiday: bit.ly/HoufNWH
Family Newsletter: bit.ly/HoufDecNews
Staff Newsletter: bit.ly/HoufFriFocus
Professional Development Tool:
    bit.ly/ELACurRev
Mini-PD Module: bit.ly/HoufTwitter
State Testing Info: bit.ly/HoufTesting
Introductions and New Year Kickoff:
    bit.ly/meetmrshouf, bit.ly/HoufNewYear
School Events: bit.ly/HoufNWH

weekly parent email. The excitement quickly grew for this event because it was nothing like we had done before. We had many patrons ask to attend the day. Also, schools from around the world reached out via Twitter to collaborate to create their own No Worksheet Holiday.

Later, I shared Smore.com with others in our building and the district and also started using it as a newsletter for both families and staff. I also branched out to use this tool for professional development, mini-PD modules, and even to get ready for state testing. The more I got to know Smore, the more I used it as a tool to build rapport, first, connecting with families and staff and then showcasing school events.

When used appropriately, technology affords us amazing opportunities to create and share information. I love Smore, but this tool is just one example of what's available. Be open to trying new apps. Experiment with new programs until you find the tech tools that work for you.

Staff Retreats and Socials

Staff retreats are a perfect way to build trust and have fun when they are correctly implemented, and we have both used them in powerful ways to connect with our teams. In a thought-provoking post on his blog, Principal Jimmy Casas shares his thoughts about retreats:

Summer Retreats: This may surprise you a bit, but when district or building leaders do not come prepared with specific agendas and a specific focus to what the retreat will entail, we risk our folks not investing in the process and therefore leaving the experience disappointed. If this experience is repeated the following year, the retreat becomes nothing more than a check mark that reflects an item taken off the summer list. And by the way, if you are going to call it a retreat, then leave the campus; include some activities that promote teamwork, bonding, and genuine investment in each other. Holding all-day meetings does not constitute a retreat.

Reading this blog post helped me (Beth) to set the tone for the organization of our 2016 summer middle-school-staff retreat. I knew that building relationships and trust would help create the foundation of an amazing school culture, so I set three simple goals for the retreat: promote teamwork, bonding, and genuine investment in each other. I typically have very few school tasks that I complete individually, but our retreat is one thing that I plan alone. I want our leadership team, including the assistant principal, to have the opportunity to be fully immersed as participants and not feel distracted by having to lead any portion of the retreat. I sent out a survey for the best date and times and then the planning began. First, I secured a location for the retreat away from school. I wanted this to feel like a real retreat! (And as Jimmy noted in his blog post, day-long meetings on campus don't count as a retreat. Plus, when you are in the school building, no matter the agenda of your time together, participants will always be thinking about what they need to be doing in their classroom or area to get ready for next year. Don't let that distraction happen! Find an off-campus location for your retreat.)

Then, the agenda began to take shape. The overarching theme of the day would be "People, Not Programs." We would have a few traditional team-building activities, and there would also be time to be completely *untraditional* in our last two activities. The invitation asked the staff to bring a snack and wear their favorite T-shirt, one that meant something to them.

I packed up early and headed to our venue. Our leadership team members showed up early, without even being asked, to help transform our area into a tropical pirate adventure land. We were ready for our crew to arrive!

The beginning of the retreat included time for informal conversations, snacks, and photo-booth pictures. The level of laughter was high within the first few minutes. Almost all of our staff attended. Custodians, cooks, teachers, secretaries, and administrators—all came together to make our school better for our students. We gathered first for a round of "Have You Ever." The directions were for the person in the middle of the circle to share who they are, what they do at the school, and why they picked the shirt they chose to wear, then a statement to get people to move around. I modeled the directions and took the first risk. Through this first activity we learned so much about each other. We found we had mountain climbers, world travelers, chefs, video gamers, and that we are much more alike than different. After the game, we split into our teams for the day. I intentionally set up teams to include a new staff member, a veteran staff member, and at least one person who was active on Twitter. The first team activity was to get out the paper and crayons and have each person draw a representation of their life story, sharing as much or as little as they would like. Because this information was a little more private, we shared these with partners, using the structure: stand up, hand up, pair up. Each staff member had the chance to share with at least five colleagues before returning to teams. We then took time to process why we did this activity. The common theme shared by staff is that our life story is what drives what we do today. Understanding where our colleagues have been helps us build trust.

Our life story is what drives what we do.

At lunch, we took team building to another level. Each staff member received an envelope that contained his or her mission for our lunch preparation. Based on the mission assignment, people got into teams: main course, sides, or desserts. Each team was provided all the necessary ingredients to create its portion of the meal. The next hour was filled with laughter and high energy as everyone got busy contributing. Each group worked to use their ingredients to create a tasty and visually appealing (per the mission guidelines) contribution to our lunch. We then sat together and enjoyed a delicious meal. And let me tell you, there is a special kind of fellowship that happens when a meal is prepared and eaten together.

After lunch, it was time for our final activity. Back in their groups, each team had forty minutes to complete as many of the scavenger hunt

STAFF RETREAT ACTIVITIES

Lunch-Prep Assignments: bit.ly/FMSretreat
Selfie Scavenger Hunt: bit.ly/2mulqrV

challenges as possible. The goal of this activity, in addition to continued teamwork, was to get into the community. We get so stuck in our own routines and buildings that we forget our students come from previous schools and have their own areas of interest. The way to record challenge completion was to Tweet out a picture of the team to our school hashtag as they did the task. I laughed (loudly) as I watched the hashtag on Twitter and kept track of points for the next forty minutes! The smiles on the faces of staff members in those pictures were pure gold! We circled up one last time to reflect. The uncertainty and nervousness from the morning was gone. We were a team and ready to enjoy the rest of the summer so that we could kick off the #BestYearYet.

Pokémon GO Staff Social

Pokémon GO became all the rage in the summer of 2016. Our own kids also became obsessed with "catching them all." My (Beth's) leadership team brainstormed the idea of a staff (and staff family) Pokémon GO night to discover what all the buzz was about before our students returned for the new school year. Our district administration was also worried about the safety implications of Pokémon GO, so we invited them along before making any decisions about putting up virtual fences around schools or banning the game entirely. We gathered in our school gym, went over some safety ground rules, and headed downtown. Watching a parade of grown people trying to catch Pokémon kept us laughing all night. Our own kids helped the adults get it figured out. We quickly found that the negative press for this game was definitely hyped up and that it was better to embrace this new technology as a school district than to ban it.

Year of Learning Blog

As a district-level administrator, thinking of ways to build relationships across the system can be a bit overwhelming, but there are several steps you can take. One of the things I (Shelley) implemented while in the assistant superintendent role was our "Year of Learning" blog. I had caught wind of the idea through a connection with George Couros who was doing something similar in his system. We started a blog with its first post on the first day of school and committed to a new post each day from members of our district community responding to the prompt "What are you learning today?" Teachers, classified staff, students, administrators, parents, and board members were all invited to share—and many participated. Every day throughout the school year, a new post went up. We had hundreds of subscribers to the email list and even more hits per day on the site. The posts sparked conversations among people across the system—people who had not previously been connected. It also sparked an incredible newspaper article in the *San Diego Union Tribune* highlighting the project and the good it was doing for the district community (bit.ly/2nCtvrL).

Staff Appreciation

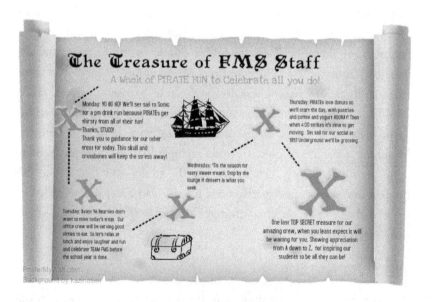

Everyone loves a day of special snacks or a bonus jeans day. My (Beth's) school has celebrated our staff with a week of PIRATE fun, complete with sweets and sodas. (See the "Treasure Map" below.) But people also love to be appreciated on a more personal level. There are so many ways you can make your crew feel special. For example, for the past two years, I (Beth) have given each member of my staff the book *P is for PIRATE* and personalized a note to match each staff member with a page in the book that best represents him/her.

I (Shelley) used a similar strategy, leaving personal notes along with bottled water and snacks on the desk of every employee on the first day of school to show my appreciation for the work everyone did to make the kickoff amazing. I have also held an annual raffle for a "free" day off where the winning teacher got to take a day off from school while I covered their class for a day.

The heartfelt thank-yous, hugs, notes, emails, Tweets, and Facebook posts of appreciation for these types of gifts are overwhelming. Indeed, the more you give, the more you get in return.

RAPPORT CHALLENGE

- What are some of the procedures or practices you have in place that may imply a lack of trust? How can you remove these barricades and give more trust to your team?

- Take some time to reflect on your relationship with staff. Which staff members do you have strong rapport with at this time? Why is that?

- Which staff members could use a rapport boost? During the next week, use some of the trust-building strategies we've shared to increase rapport with one or two staff members.

 Share your thoughts, ideas, and artifacts with the *Lead Like a PIRATE* community using the #LeadLAP hashtag.

Navigating the C's of Change

Ask & Analyze

Compass to Guide You

Clarity:

Mission and objectives are clear and everyone understands. Can explain the "why" of everything.

Capacity:

Growth mindset and open to new things. Has a learner's mentality.

Cannonballs to Avoid

Cryptic:

Unable to clearly identify what you are about or your mission. Can't clearly delineate the "why" of what is going on.

Confined:

Small-minded and fixed mindset. Doesn't want change because it's too much work.

ASK & ANALYZE

I (Shelley) shared earlier some of the things that went wrong when we rolled out our new teaching protocol and the resulting checklist. Analyzing both what went well (and there definitely were things that went well) and what went wrong in the implementation of this initiative helped me as I planned new initiatives in my role as assistant superintendent. One of those initiatives was the transition to Common Core State Standards. Reflecting on what had and hadn't worked in the past helped me develop a set of guiding questions that my team and I then used to plan and lead the overhaul of our curriculum and instruction. The questions we kept at the forefront of our thinking as we moved forward were these:

- How will we build the new initiative into our work over time?

- How will we make connections between the new initiative and work we are already doing?

- How will we build capacity of our Educational Leadership Team (district and site leaders) to lead the new initiative?

- What do leaders need to know and be able to do to successfully to lead this initiative at their schools?

- How will we collaborate with our teachers' union as we move this initiative forward?

- How will we build shared leadership and ownership of the new initiative?

- What will teachers need to know and be able to do to be successful with the new implementation and how will we support them in their new learning?

- How will we ensure that every person impacted by the new initiative has some voice and choice so they feel this is something we have done with them, not to them?

- What system will we put in place to ensure we are gathering authentic and honest feedback about how things are going and the support people need? How will we use this feedback to make alterations as we move forward?

- How will we monitor implementation in a respectful way and use this data to refine the work over time?

Using these questions as our guidelines helped us plan thoughtfully and purposefully every step of the way. We were able to generate a long-term plan and make immediate adjustments based on feedback. Asking the right questions and revisiting them often kept us focused and held us accountable to doing good work that the people in our system could support.

PIRATE leaders ask many thoughtful questions of themselves and of others, and they are skillful at analyzing all of the data that comes at them. When there are obstacles and challenges, they don't throw up their hands in defeat. Instead, they ask probing questions, dig deep to get to the root of the issue, and actively seek solutions. Hungry for answers, they reach out to others for advice. As leaders, if we want to transform our schools and our districts, it really does start with asking better questions.

Ask Questions That Transform

In John Maxwell's book *Good Leaders Ask Great Questions: Your Foundation for Successful Leadership* (a book that should be on every leader's shelf), he shares eight reasons that it is important for leaders to be intentional about the questions they ask:

1. You only get answers to the questions you ask.

2. Questions unlock and open doors that otherwise remain closed.

3. Questions are the most effective means of connecting with people.

4. Questions cultivate humility.

5. Questions help us to engage others in conversation.

6. Questions allow us to build better ideas.

7. Questions give us a different perspective.

8. Questions challenge mindsets and get us out of ruts.

If we want to get out of ruts, engage students and staff members alike, spark innovation, and build a culture of inclusion and excitement—if we want to help teachers light up the skies of their classrooms with more wonder and wow . . . more *bang* and *boom*—then we need to make sure we're asking the right types of questions. We need to ask questions that invite curiosity, encourage more questions, and help us find meaningful, relevant answers.

"What will we do on the first day of school this year?" Think about this question for a moment. You have probably asked this same question or a version of it every year you have served as an educator. Now think

about how you and your team typically answer it. Oftentimes the answers are filled with the rituals and routines of starting a school year. We answer with information about going over the rules and schedules, a review of the procedures. Answers focus on duty assignments, procedures for staff, onboarding students and parents, and teaching kids where to line up for lunch. We aren't suggesting that these aren't all important things to plan for, but what if we changed the question to this...

What can we do on the first day of school that is so wildly engaging and fun that our students are knocking down the doors to get in on day two?

Now what happens? What comes to mind as you try to answer this question? We are guessing you have moved away from thoughts about rules, procedures, and routines.

Good questions inform; great questions transform.

One of the things we like to do is challenge leaders to elevate their questions by taking their traditional questions—those that have become routine and that their crew can answer in their sleep—and kicking them up a notch! Because as John Maxwell has taught us, *good questions inform; great questions transform.*

If you really want to transform your school, its culture, and the way you and your staff members work and learn, start asking better questions. Traditional questions elicit traditional responses, but the transformed questions inspire a new way of thinking. Take a look at the examples of transformed questions on the opposite page.

PIRATE leaders ask questions like these—questions that challenge the status quo, inspire outside-the-textbook experiences, and encourage new ways of thinking about practice. They also ask questions that encourage collaboration and teamwork, questions such as "What do you think?" "How can I help?" or "What obstacles can I get out of your way?"

Traditional Question	Transformed Questions
What are your goals for this year?	What magic do you want to create in your classroom this year? How can I help? What memories do you want to create for students in your class this year? How do you plan to do that? What's something you have always wanted to do in your class, but haven't tried yet? How can I help make that happen?
What strategies will you use to engage students in your lesson?	What could you do to create a "buzz" about next week's lesson so your students are excited and engaged before they even walk in the door? What will you do during your lesson that will inspire students to bubble over with excitement when parents or friends ask them, "What did you do in school today?"
What is the agenda for your next staff meeting?	How can you find out what your teachers want to learn? How could you personalize professional development to create experiences that would get your staff running into meetings, not out? How could you transform your adult learning spaces to immediately and positively change the atmosphere and vibe of the room? What hooks could you use before the meeting to get staff pumped up about the topic?

Not only do PIRATE leaders ask transformative questions, but they also work to get really good at listening to the responses and using them as feedback to shape the culture of the school or district.

Analyze Outcomes and Feedback

Likewise, PIRATE leaders hone their analytical skills. We need to be able to diagnose what's going on in our schools and in our classrooms. We need to be able to determine whether a program is or isn't working, or if the professional learning we have offered is making the impact we had hoped for. We need to analyze who needs support in what area. As PIRATE leaders, we are hungry for data of all kinds—from learning assessments to observation, dialogue, and a whole host of other ways to get information.

Asking, listening, analyzing, reflecting, and learning are all essential to your role as a leader. When things go well, ask, "Why did it go well?" Identify the actions that took place to make an activity, meeting, or initiative successful—because success does not happen by accident. It happens as a result of strategic and intentional decisions. An equally valuable exercise is to identify the reason something *doesn't* go as you'd hoped it would. Make time to reflect on the data you've gathered, the decisions you made, and then learn from the missteps and the mistakes. As Dave says in *Teach Like a PIRATE*, "There isn't failure, only feedback." What feedback are you getting on the decisions being made in your school? How are you using this feedback to become better today than you were yesterday?

Asking, listening, analyzing, reflecting, and learning are all essential to your role as a leader.

PIRATE leaders must also constantly analyze the practices we expect of our staff. One example for me (Beth) was the mandated posting of learning targets. This was an expectation I had of my staff when I moved into my role at the middle school. Each staff member had a dry-erase board outside their door that stated: *Today I Will Learn* . . . Let's just say the kids were not beating down the doors to get in with whatever state standard was written on the board. Who can blame them?! The feedback I got from talking with students was that simply posting the target wasn't effective if nothing else was done with what was written. So rather than bore them by posting standard mandates, the teachers turned their boards into hook marquees. Now, teachers work to capture students' attention *before* they even get in the room.

Another opportunity to listen to and analyze feedback came when parents and students of my district told me the transition from our elementary schools to our middle school was not adequate. They told us they felt rushed during open house for new sixth graders. With that feedback, the school's counseling team and I explored ideas and asked lots of questions to our students, parents, and teachers. We analyzed the pros and cons of our past practices and ultimately designed a partial-day "camp" experience for our kids to help ease our newest students into middle school. The event helped familiarize students with the school, which alleviated some of their stress. Additionally, one of our counselors reached out for community support so that we could furnish each child with a T-shirt and give students the opportunity to enjoy a meal in the cafeteria before the first day of school. Here's the flyer we used to engage the sponsors for our Back-to-School Camp: bit.ly/HoufHelpWanted.

Believe it or not, figuring out how the cafeteria works is actually the number-one fear of new middle schoolers. Having a meal together allowed us to build community and relieve that fear. And the T-shirt, which included their graduation year, bolstered school pride and helped set the vision and long-term goal of scholastic success. We had almost 100 percent student participation in the camp. And when it was all over, we took time to ask questions and analyze next steps. This new annual tradition has resulted in massive, positive changes to our sixth-grade culture, as well as with the parents who are new to the middle-school campus.

ASK AND ANALYZE CHALLENGE

- Think of an initiative you are leading at your school or in your district. What are the guiding questions you are using to drive you and help you move forward? And if you don't have any, write some down now.

- What are some of the routine questions you ask your staff? How can you transform them to get better, more meaningful answers?

- Take time to reflect on a recent school activity or staff event. What went well, and why? What didn't go well? What could you do differently next time to get better results?

Share your thoughts, ideas, and artifacts with the *Lead Like a PIRATE* community using the #LeadLAP hashtag.

Navigating the C's of Change

Transformation

Compass to Guide You

Courageous:

Willing to take risks for growth and make a stand in order to make your school better.

Cannonballs to Avoid

Cowardly:

Only takes small steps and mediocrity is acceptable. Not willing to fight for what's right even knowing that it's wrong.

TRANSFORMATION

Transformation is much more than using the skills, resources and technology. It's all about the habits of the mind.
—Malcolm Gladwell, keynote, INBOUND 2014

If you do what you've always done, you'll get what you've always gotten.
—Anthony Robbins

When moving to the middle school, one of the first decisions the staff and I (Beth) made was to begin the year in a way that was unlike anything ever done before in order to showcase the changes that had been made since the spring. Back to School Like a PIRATE was ready to happen! The leadership team and I worked together to create a staff challenge to teach the most amazing lessons the first week of school. No rules, no boring beginnings—just pure passion and enthusiasm for the year's learning. I shared this idea in my blog and had nearly 8,000 views from educators around the world. Fulton Middle School wasn't the only place where people were ready to transform the traditional back-to-school plans. I also created a shared document to which all educators could contribute.

To help establish a team mentality, the staff would dress in high-school football jerseys and hold a kickoff assembly in the gym to begin the best year ever.

The big day arrived and the energy was palpable. All of the staff and student council lined the sidewalk to the school and greeted students with high fives and cheers. The energy was through the roof! The assembly kicked off with a welcome to students and then a dance-off between the two new administrators. The students looked as if they were in awe that their teachers and principals were laughing and enjoying school. This became the new norm for our school. The first week of school continued with the passion and enthusiasm for learning that was spread to students. Trust and relationship building were the continued focus as staff contacted the parents of every student on their roster to give a positive phone call or email. A positive-referral system was rolled out for students. Staff could nominate a student for going above and beyond, the referral was hung on the brag board, and a family member would be contacted. This was another culture shift for our school. This positive-referral system became so popular that students wanted to be a part of the nomination as well. A student team organized this and rolled it out to the student body.

BACK-TO-SCHOOL LIKE A PIRATE

Blog Post: bit.ly/BTSLAP

Collaborative Idea Doc: bit.ly/BTSDoc

PIRATE leaders want to make a significant difference, a notable contribution, and transform the lives of their students. They have a clear vision about where they want to go and why it is an important journey for people to take with them. They have high expectations and create a healthy sense of urgency around the most important work, and they are skillful in managing and leading change. They know that great schools can change communities and change the lives of generations. They believe in the moral imperative of providing students with an amazing set of educational opportunities, they are clear in defining what these are, and then they orchestrate the experience.

Transformation in Action!

If we are truly serious about creating the culture of getting our students and staff running in rather than out, we have to be willing to transform our daily practices. We can't be satisfied with mediocre or status quo. We have to be relentless each day if we are going to take traditional education to new heights for our staff and students. "Whatever it takes" is the mantra of PIRATE leaders ready to make a difference.

From Parent/Teacher to Student-Led Conferences

Historically, less than 50 percent of families attended parent/teacher conferences at my (Beth's) middle school. That's a huge drop off in attendance compared to the elementary setting, where parent participation in conferences was typically 99–100 percent. To increase family involvement and help fulfill our school's mission of empowering students, our leadership team—in conjunction with the parent/community engagement focus team—decided to transform these events. They researched the use of student-led conferences and ultimately found a way to give students ownership of the conference while improving communication between teachers and families.

Our first goal was to be sure that our staff, students, and parents had a clear communication of the *why* of our new procedures, as well as the *how*. We developed digital, print, and video directions for all stakeholders. We then implemented our new

SAMPLE DOCS FOR STUDENT-LED CONFERENCES

Staff Directions for Fall Student-Led Conferences: bit.ly/StaffSLC

Student Organizer for Fall Evaluations and Grades: bit.ly/FMSSLC

Video Newsletter Explaining Fall Student-Led Conferences: bit.ly/SLCYouTube

Spring Conference Info: bit.ly/SLConferences

structure. Our students first recorded their grades, as well as an area of strength and growth potential, in each class on an advanced organizer. The teachers initialed the students' grades after having a reflective conversation with each student. Students and parents then had options of up to nine events to participate in during the student-led conference times. Each student who attended would also be able to eat lunch outside on our football field with a little recess time. (It's amazing how much middle school misses recess!)

More than 85 percent of the school families attended these fall conferences. This was a new record and celebration for the school. Parents wanted to be engaged in their children's education, but we had to develop the correct means to make this happen.

Afterward, we took time to reflect on changes that could be made before we did this again in the spring. The first thing we realized was that we needed to spend time helping our students identify specific goals as well as areas of growth. We saw a lot of "read more," "write more," "stay out of trouble," but what do those phrases really mean for growth to occur? We spent time over the year working on this and then held a very similar conference format in the spring; however, we set a new goal of 90 percent attendance. Students would again earn lunch and recess outside, and I added that I would spend the night in the trophy case if they could truly meet this goal. With the dedication of our students, parents, and staff, we not only hit our goal—we crushed it at 96 percent attendance. *Wow!* This was such a celebration for our school! And yes, I spent the night in the trophy case, and it is a night I will never forget. Seeing the kids' faces the next morning definitely made it worth it!

Rethinking Intervention: WIN (What I Need)

Response to Intervention has become common practice in districts across the United States. Fulton Middle School had tried several different models of intervention blocks to respond to the variety of needs of its students. Unfortunately, each model met only the needs of specific groups of students; no one model met every student's needs.

Before starting as principal in the fall of 2015, I (Beth) asked for feedback from students, staff, and parents regarding the current intervention block, which was called SIT (structured intervention time). I also observed the block in action and saw that what was dubbed an intervention block was, in reality, a continuation of Tier 1 instruction. All students in each grade level received the same information; there was no differentiation to meet the needs of learners. Not surprisingly, engagement was low and behavior issues were high.

My leadership team and I began brainstorming ways to individualize intervention time so students would get what they truly needed. Together, we established the parameters for what we now call WIN (What I Need) Time. Using the foundational work of Austin Buffum, Mike Mattos, and Chris Weber in *Pyramid Response to Intervention: RTI, Professional Learning Communities, and How to Respond When Kids Don't Learn*, we outlined the why, what, and how of WIN.

Brainstorm ways to individualize intervention time so students can get what they truly need.

Individualization is the key to WIN Time: Students are provided with opportunities to get additional help in the specific areas in which they are struggling. They are also encouraged to identify their interests and possible career choices using Thrively.com, which uses a strengths inventory to create a personalized portfolio of online field trips, apps, videos, and games that match their passions.

After our students took their first benchmark assessments, the leadership team set up groups based on need. Students who didn't need a specific intervention were placed in a Genius Hour group where they had the opportunity to explore personal passions and interests. Our technology teacher took the lead for this group and developed a structure for the Genius Hour WIN Time. She then trained our staff and did a big kickoff on the first day of WIN in the gymnasium. More than 300 students were fired up and ready to take charge of their learning.

The first WIN Time lasted three weeks. Every teacher, counselor, and principal had an assignment, and during this time, we all monitored progress, and gave feedback. Together, we focused on living out the school's mission of Educating, Engaging, and Empowering ALL Learners at Escalating Levels. Throughout the WIN Time sessions, students received extra instruction in all core and exploratory areas. They also created robots, learned coding, became "mad scientists," and learned new languages.

We had transformed intervention time from the ineffective, one-size-fits-all model of years past into something empowering. The students helped design the plan for the next session, which followed a similar structure and included student input on the topics, in addition to Genius Hour for extension opportunities. We continued tweaks after session two, which helped to make session three even better. We added mental health and behavior interventions during the third session of WIN. Also in session three of WIN, twenty students helped to create our school's first makerspace. Students were able to move more fluidly from intervention to extension as they caught up in classes and mastered concepts. The end result was that student engagement and ownership of learning skyrocketed!

For the remainder of the year, grade levels and departments took ownership for the intervention and enrichment needs. Using Google Apps, we created a virtual data wall to help keep track of individual student needs and benchmark information, as well as unit pre-test/post-test data for essential learning outcomes. In addition to academic data, we tracked attendance and office referrals so that we could be sure we were providing what truly was needed to meet the needs of our kids. We also added students' strengths to the data. Using this data, our WIN time was able to become fluid. Students could change daily, if needed. Instead of relying solely on benchmark assessments and putting kids in an intervention for an allotted time no matter what, we differentiated intervention time and activities to meet the needs of our students.

Design Uncommon Experiences to Transform Learning

Provide an uncommon experience for your students, and they will reward you with an uncommon effort and attitude.
—Dave Burgess, *Teach Like a PIRATE*

When we, as PIRATE leaders, transform our leadership practices, the effect ripples across our campuses. As I (Beth) mentioned at the opening of this book, I came back from the conference in the summer of 2014 a changed person—a PIRATE leader—in all I did, which resulted in a glimmer of change throughout our building that semester. But the day before Thanksgiving break a realization hit me: The change was no longer a glimmer, it had exploded like a lightning bolt across our campus. The spark that had been growing brighter seemed to suddenly catch fire. I had woken up that morning with the normal excitement of the approaching Thanksgiving holiday. I looked forward to a day at school before a long weekend to relax and celebrate with family and friends. Little did I know I would leave that night with a renewed sense of purpose, passion, and priorities because of the experiences provided to me by our amazing staff and students.

The morning began in a classroom designed to look like an Author's Café set in Paris. Students shared writing projects and pastries with parents and special guests. What writers! Their hard work was evident in each piece.

Next door, teams of students were being challenged to create their own colonies to see who could survive. This required collaboration, planning, and risk taking by both the students and the teacher, and not to mention amazing effort!

As the day unfolded, I transformed from principal to news reporter, showcasing the amazing things happening in our building. Teachers most definitely provided *uncommon* experiences which evoked uncommon effort and attitude from each and every student. Not only was each of these classroom activities directly tied to curriculum objectives, but students and teachers were deeply engaged and having fun! And the best thing was that this day was not a planned building "holiday"—the activities were the result of our teachers' creativity and hard work.

I ventured across the hall, where students were given a set amount of money to plan a Thanksgiving meal. What an authentic way of practicing decimal skills! They were furiously working with a partner to comb local advertisements to create delicious meals and spend every penny. I think students were a little shocked at how expensive it is to plan a big meal! My morning walk continued, and I visited another classroom where students had the task of writing in the time of the Pilgrims, complete with period dialect and special "aged" paper. The next classroom had been transformed into the colonial period, and teams of students had been challenged to design and build a replica shelter that would have been found during this time period. Farther down the hallway, I could hear the theme song from Mission Impossible playing.

Our kindergarten and first graders transformed our cafetorium into the first Thanksgiving feast. The students learned about working together and gratitude from the amazing example set forth by their teachers. The smiles, hugs, and thankful hearts reminded me that, despite all of the negativity we see in the news, we really live in a wonderful world.

As the feast concluded, I headed back to the hallway. I was definitely not disappointed as I moved into second-grade classrooms. A food "hook" awaited me in one room where students were churning their own butter. Next door, students were designing, making, and trading jewelry as they had learned about in their Native American unit—what energy! And the best thing, these amazing eight year olds gave me the full rundown of the purpose and importance of each step in the process. They completely owned their learning! In another hall, a fourth-grade class welcomed me to a publishing party. Students eagerly and passionately shared stories with me.

By then, lunch duty was calling and I headed back to the cafetorium. I know many teachers and principals don't enjoy lunch duty, but I have to tell you: It is so great to have time to talk with kids, connect, and build rapport. It was also a time for our students to see how we all work together to serve meals, clean tables, and synergize as a staff.

Back to classrooms in the afternoon, and I was continually amazed at the levels of student engagement—on the day before break, no less! I witnessed third graders taking over the teaching in the classroom. More food hooks and taking time to reflect on thankfulness. I watched flashlights being built in one fourth-grade class and sound-effect storytelling in another. I could go on and on sharing about the uncommonly engaging lessons I saw taking place that day.

My day concluded by recognizing our positive referrals for the day over the P.A. system, leading the principal dance party, and then sending off our students with high fives and smiles as they headed home for a long Thanksgiving break. It was a fantastic ending to an amazing day!

As a leader, it is so easy to let the noise of our profession drown out the main thing—the awesome experiences happening in our schools to support learning. The *main thing* doesn't happen in the principal's office, it happens live throughout our buildings all day long. As we model, appreciate, and showcase these awesome experiences, they replicate. The next thing you know, you have a school full of PIRATEs, and that's a great thing!

Transformation Challenge

- Take a moment to reflect and list below the programs, initiatives, traditional activities that happen on your campus.

- Push yourself to ask more powerful questions that will help you transform them to have more bam! and less blah.

- Write down your transformed task and prepare to implement it!

- Share your thoughts, ideas, and artifacts with the Lead Like a PIRATE community using the #LeadLAP hashtag.

TRADITIONAL LEADERSHIP TASKS	ASK & ANALYZE	TRANSFORMATION
	How can this be more *bam!* and less *blah?*	

Share your thoughts, ideas, and artifacts with the *Lead Like a PIRATE* community using the #LeadLAP hashtag.

Navigating the C's of Change

Enthusiasm

Compass to Guide You

Captivating:

Willing to step outside the box to engage and have fun.

Cannonballs to Avoid

Clinical:

Over-analyzing every situation and decision causing paralysis by analysis. Afraid to try something new.

ENTHUSIASM

Enthusiasm moves the world.
—Arthur Balfour

Serious learning can be seriously fun.
—Quinn Rollins, *Play Like a Pirate*

We're lucky in education in that we really get at least two fresh starts. (If you work on a trimester calendar, you get three new beginnings!) To kick off the second semester at Fulton Middle School, we really celebrate the New Year. We capitalize on the concepts of new beginnings, setting goals, and giving our students a fresh start—something we all need!

One example of celebrating the New Year is when the FMS Staff welcomes students back by (literally) rolling out the red carpet and hosting a New Year's Party. Staff dresses in formal, "tacky prom" attire. When our students get off the buses, we overhear so many students saying things like, "What in the world are they up to now?"

With a little effort and a ton of enthusiasm, we transformed what could have been one of those I-don't-wanna-go-back-to-school days into an I'm-so-excited! day.

> ## RING IN THE NEW YEAR
>
> See the New Year's celebration invitations we sent to students' families and our staff.
>
> **Families:** bit.ly/FMSHNY
>
> **Staff:** smore.com/oyuzf-happy-new-year

Our New Year's celebration is certainly a memorable event, but students (and teachers) benefit from regular doses of enthusiasm. Starting the morning on the right note can make all the difference between a good day and a terrible-horrible-no-good-very-bad day. Think about it: For some students (and staff!), mornings can be the hardest times to muster energy, much less enthusiasm. One way we pump up the excitement at FMS is to make morning bus duty *Enthusiasm Central*. Each child is greeted with the kind of enthusiasm that lets them know they matter. Regardless of what may have happened before 7:30 a.m., the morning bus-duty crew commits to making the magic happen! From dance parties to karaoke, I (Beth) and my teachers and staff do whatever it takes to put smiles on the faces of our middle schoolers.

A principal colleague we know from another school announces students' names as they get off the buses—as if they're honored guests being welcomed to a formal event. However you choose to show your enthusiasm, the point is to make sure your students and staff know that you are excited and honored that you get to share your day with them.

When you intentionally and regularly create that kind of enthusiasm, the net result is a school where kids want to come to learn and grow. And that's when you really change lives.

PIRATE leaders infuse enthusiasm into their work. They *bring it* every day, and they are committed to being *on*. They are the champions and cheerleaders of their schools and champions and cheerleaders of those who work and learn there. They celebrate successes both big and small. You know enthusiastic leaders when you see them. They are the ones who can bring you up when you are down; they help you reignite your fire when it is starting to burn out; they point out how you have contributed and made a difference; they smile; they laugh; they engage; they commit.

Fake It till You Feel It!

Dave says in his *Teach Like a PIRATE* seminars that one difference between enthusiasm and passion is that you can't fake passion. But sometimes, when you don't feel totally *on* or excited about your day, you can "fake it until you make it" with enthusiasm for the benefit of your staff and students. PIRATE leaders know that they have to bring energy and excitement to each day, no matter what.

As leaders, we have a responsibility to model positivity and enthusiasm. We can't expect our staff and students to be enthusiastic about things that we are not enthusiastic about. We do this by being excited about everything that school is about. We cheer when students arrive. We throw a party when teachers and students take risks. We celebrate mistakes as well as successes, and we celebrate the learning that goes along with these. Most of all, our enthusiasm for our jobs and for our schools is evident in every facet of our leadership. This also holds true for the things we may not look forward to doing as leaders, such as rolling out newly mandated initiatives or curriculum changes at the state level (again). We don't always have a choice in the day-to-day work we do, but we definitely have a choice in the way that we do it.

Each fall, we are assigned mandated topics that must be covered with staff due to insurance regulations. These topics range from harassment to confidentiality to blood-borne pathogens. Exciting, huh? These are important topics, but definitely not the most engaging, especially when teachers are trying to get rooms ready for open house and lessons planned for newly arriving students. Beth's district fulfills this mandate by making videos and releasing them six weeks before school starts so that staff can view them as they have time. The email accompanying the videos is intentionally funny and inviting. The point is, you can take a tough topic and make it harder, or you can reframe the situation to try to make it better.

PIRATE leaders continually ask good questions and analyze school practices, looking for what works and what isn't effective. Enthusiasm is often the missing element to engagement. With a little creativity, enthusiasm, and—yes—at the risk of looking silly, you can take something that is traditionally ineffective (aka boring), kick the energy up a notch, and make it meaningful, even valuable. For instance, when your school has new rules or guidelines to share with staff or students, you can announce them in an assembly or over the PA while everyone's eyes glaze over in boredom, or you can send home a letter that may or may not get read before ending up in the recycle bin. Posting a funny meme may get a few people's attention, but even that will likely be forgotten quickly.

> ## Enthusiasm is often the missing element to engagement.

So how can you get people to pay attention so you can get your message across? Get creative! I (Beth) and my assistant principal, inspired by late-night television and with the help of their school's tech facilitator, created a (fun and memorable) "Carpool Karaoke" video (bit.ly/FMSCPKaraoke) to share the new school-year procedures with students and their families.

Have Some Fun!

It's okay—actually, it's *encouraged*—to add an element of fun in the workday. As the leader, you are the emotional guide for others in your school. When you are stressed, you project that to your staff, students, and parents. If someone asks, "Are you okay?" it's time to recalibrate your energy level. When a staff member or student comes to you excited about a new idea, it's critical that your reaction—both in words *and* body language—stoke (rather than extinguish) the flames of their enthusiasm. Make deliberate, daily choices to help keep the fires going.

Choose to be contagious with enthusiasm! Life is too short to be in a job that sucks the enjoyment out of everything. Your attitude spreads to those around you. When you act a little (or, maybe a lot) zany, you embolden your staff to loosen up and have fun. And guess what: When your teachers are having fun, they'll pass it right along to the students. The next thing you know, your culture is one built on positivity and the enjoyment of learning.

I (Beth) have had the opportunity to witness the contagious effects of enthusiasm firsthand. One wing of our school does "Karaoke Friday" during passing periods. Teachers set the scene, complete with a karaoke machine, disco ball, and flashing lights. Students (and staff!) literally run to this area to be a part of the fun. It has become a regular and much-anticipated part of each week! This has led to a teacher in a different hallway bringing his guitar to pump up students as they transition between periods. Kids dance down the hallway on their way to class.

Another teacher started a daily Twitter challenge to showcase the amazing happenings in each of our classrooms. Her enthusiasm for building our school culture spreads daily to her colleagues. She and her team of seventh-grade ELA teachers have encouraged the students to share their voices on Twitter. Imagine my surprise to see seventh graders on the first day of school participating in a Twitter chat. Wow!

It is more common than not in our building to see teachers in costume to add that extra *bam*! to the lesson plan. We have had Pokémon's Ash Ketchum, the crew from *The Wizard of Oz*, and Susan B. Anthony to help crush that close reading. Characters regularly make guest appearances: Mrs. Slope has stopped in with her children Rise and Run. Mr. and Mrs. Wilderness lead students through a survival unit to explore the new world. I never know who I will see walking the halls of our building! When teachers are empowered to take risks and think beyond the textbook and curriculum guides, the possibilities are truly endless!

During our Lead Like a PIRATE workshops, we have had some educators ask if kids will take them seriously if they show their fun, even silly side while teaching and leading. Our answer is a great big YES! And they'll be engaged while learning. Listen, as leaders, we must take our jobs very seriously, but never ourselves. No one enjoys learning and working in an environment that is serious all the time. Learning and fun shouldn't be mutually exclusive. As Dave says, we are in the life-changing business! Lukewarm lessons and status-quo leadership are a recipe for bland, forgettable learning. Kick your enthusiasm up a notch and watch it ripple to all around!

Enthusiasm Challenge

As Todd Whitaker says, "When the principal sneezes, the whole school catches a cold."

- If your attitude is contagious, what are you spreading to your staff? Is this a good thing? How could you ensure that the Jolly Roger is flying proudly through the toughest of times?

- How do you start and end each day as a leader? Does it evoke enthusiasm? How could you make a change to ramp up the positivity?

- Nothing beats in-person enthusiasm, but never underestimate the power of technology. Choose one way to showcase the enthusiasm in your school through social media, digital newsletters, videos, etc. and try it this week!

- Plan ahead! Is there something you can prepare or plan now that will give your school an extra dose of enthusiasm during a time of year where it is traditionally low?

Share your thoughts, ideas, and artifacts with the *Lead Like a PIRATE* community using the #LeadLAP hashtag.

X Marks the Spot: Leadership Treasure

We've just shown you how the core concepts of PIRATE apply to and enhance your roles as an educational leader. In this section, we want to share with you some of the things we treasure as leaders. What follows are some of the thoughts, ideas, and guiding principles that help define us as leaders. They help shape us and make us who we are.

Everybody knows that pirates seek treasure. In fact, it is their primary pursuit; they are willing to risk everything to get it! The type of treasure you seek as a PIRATE leader defines the True North of your educational compass.

SET YOUR COMPASS

A vision builds trust, collaboration, interdependence, motivation, and mutual responsibility for success. Vision helps people make smart choices because their decisions are made with the end result in mind. Vision allows us to act from a proactive stance, moving toward what we want. Vision empowers and excites us to reach for what we truly desire.
—Ken Blanchard, *Leading at a Higher Level*

The real path to greatness, it turns out, requires simplicity and diligence. It requires clarity, not instant illumination. It demands each of us to focus on what is vital—and to eliminate all of the extraneous distractions.
—Jim Collins, *Good to Great*

Most leaders think they are focused, that they have a clear direction, and that their team is on board. An activity I (Shelley) love to do when working with school teams is to ask everyone to take a moment to reflect individually on this question: "What is the most important work you are focused on right now as a school team to improve student learning?" I require them to write down their answers and when they're done, I ask everyone to share, one at a time, what they wrote exactly—word for word. The principal shares last. A lack of consistency among answers—with some of them being drastically different from what the principal wrote down—is not uncommon when we do this exercise. But that inconsistency always surprises the leaders. The activity gives us a great jumping-off point to talk about the schools' collective vision and the clarity with which it is communicated.

It is almost cliché to talk about vision and mission in schools. Almost every school has a vision and/or mission statement. Some schools and systems are dedicated to living out the vision and mission statements that hang upon their walls. Everyone—from the custodial crew, to the students, to the administrative team—can repeat the school's mantra. That's great, and it's also rare. More often than not, if you ask people about their school or district's vision or primary focus, you will get as many different answers as the number of people you ask. If you want to set sail with your crew and chart a new course for your school or district, then everyone needs to have the same map and a compass that points them in the same direction—otherwise your ship will simply sink.

> **If a man does not know to what port he is steering, no wind is favorable to him.**
> —Seneca, *Epistle LXXI*

Several great books and resources discuss, in depth, the concepts of vision, focus, and clarity as being integral to a leader's ability to make positive, impactful change in a system. So we won't spend too much time here restating the need for them. It is worth noting, however, that a long-term vision can be your driving force as a PIRATE leader. As a leader, you have to know what you want for your school or district, not just this year but also in the years to come. You have to get crystal clear about what you and your crew need to do this year, this month, this week, tomorrow, and today to help you get where you want to go. Breaking down the vision into actionable steps that you and your team can focus on with intensity will help ensure you find your ultimate treasure. You'll also need to stay the course and push toward your goal with an unwavering commitment. New, innovative, exciting ideas are presented to educational leaders daily, so you must be relentless about filtering out ideas that don't support your long-term vision.

> *You have to decide what your highest priorities are and have the courage—pleasantly, smilingly, non-apologetically— to say "no" to other things. And the way you do that is by having a bigger "yes" burning inside. The enemy of the "best" is often the "good."*
> —Stephen R. Covey, *The 7 Habits of Highly Effective People*

Focus can be difficult to master. We know that, as educators, you are responsible for so much. You are expected to make sure all of the content standards in all subject areas are taught to students at all levels of learning. You have to teach language and content to students learning English. You also have to integrate character education, help students learn how to "say no to drugs," promote anti-bullying campaigns, ensure your students develop patriotism and a sense of civic responsibility—and the list goes on! If you feel overwhelmed with the awesome responsibility of all you have to do, well, you aren't alone.

A colleague once used this memorable analogy in her quest to be more focused:

> *When I think about how to focus at my school, it helps me to think about how I clean my house—every room is important and at some point in time needs a little bit of attention. But my kitchen needs to be cleaned every day. After every meal, I put things away, do the dishes, and wipe down the table, the counters, and the sink. I can almost always put off the dusting or the vacuuming one more day, but my kitchen can never wait until tomorrow.*

As a PIRATE leader, it is critical that you help your team take a look around the rooms in your "educational house" and find the equivalent of your "kitchen"—that thing that will need your time and attention every day. We have all heard the saying that if we try to do too many things, we are not doing any of them well. This truth plays out all too often in education. If you are going to find educational treasure, you need to identify what matters most—you have to know what you are searching for and then be relentless in your pursuit of it. Spend the majority of your time working on obtaining it.

Not only do you need to be crystal clear about your highest priorities, you must communicate them *incessantly*. Never let an opportunity to make reference to your vision, focus, or goals pass you by. Be intentional about constantly pointing out the things that are moving your school or district forward on your journey, and, when necessary, help your team members recalculate if they get a bit off course.

Focus Challenge

- Spend some time reflecting on your focus. Pull out and review all of the relevant documents (i.e., board goals and priorities, your student-achievement plan, Title I plan, Title III plan, etc.).
- Determine what your most important work is and create a document that clarifies it on paper. Use these three criteria:
  1. It has to be aligned to work you are already engaged in—no new initiatives.
  2. It has to be limited to four or fewer areas of focus.
  3. It has to fit onto one page in an easily accessible and clear format.

This is *not* an easy task and it may require you to review pages and pages of documents. But it is a great task that forces you to think about every aspect of your work and its impact on student learning and culture. It causes you to evaluate the connections between different pieces of your work and to make decisions about where a piece of work might "fit." For example, should technology be its own focus, or should it be something you use to help you achieve a different focus? It also causes you to think about what you maybe shouldn't do at all.

To see an example of how an overall focus can be broken down into specific, measurable goals and corresponding tasks, check out the "Leading the Learning" PDF here: bit.ly/2nqpesg.

 Share your thoughts, ideas, and artifacts with the *Lead Like a PIRATE* community using the #LeadLAP hashtag.

Avoid the Blame Game

We may have all come on different ships, but we're in the same boat now.
—Dr. Martin Luther King Jr.

Definition of leadership: Leadership is getting results in a way that inspires trust.
—Stephen M. R. Covey, *The Speed of Trust*

When we learn how to work together versus against each other, things might start getting better.
—Alex Elle

If only the teachers would . . .
If only the principal would . . .
If the students weren't so . . .
If the parents would just . . .
If the district would stop making us . . .

L eaders do it! Teachers do it. Staff members and parents do it. We point fingers. We blame. It can't be us, so it must be them. Blaming is a culture that exists in too many schools and school systems, and quite frankly, it's toxic. It gets in the way of creating the kinds of schools where all people thrive. How many times have you sat in a leadership meeting and heard principals complain about teachers? When you were a teacher, how often did you or other teachers you know complain about admin or the "district"? How much time and energy does blaming and complaining consume? We have both witnessed and experienced systems where an "us" vs. "them" mentality wasted countless hours of time and energy. Rather than channeling their collective energy and directing it to something positive for their schools, people committed to fighting against each other.

A core value we hold true—one that helps shape the daily work we do as leaders—is the idea that we are all on the same team. And as a team, we can accomplish great things. Being a leader of a great team requires that you highly value each individual member of your team. As a leader, when you look at each person on your team—we mean really look at each one of them—what do you see? Do you see what frustrates you? What makes you crazy? What you don't like? What you wish they wouldn't do?

Or do you see what you appreciate? What they do that makes an impact? What you admire about them and the talents they have to contribute?

How you perceive the people on your team directly influences how you treat them, what you expect of them, what you believe they can accomplish. If you don't believe in them, how can you expect to lead them?

In John Wooden's (arguably one of the best team builders of our time) book: *Leadership Game Plan for Success*, he says this:

> Over and over, I have taught that we all have a certain potential, unique to each one of us. A unique potential also exists for every team. My responsibility as a leader—and yours—is to make the utmost effort to bring forth that potential. When this occurs, you have achieved success. Then, perhaps when circumstances come together, we may find that we are very competitive, perhaps even number one.

It is my belief that when this occurs—being number one, winning—it is simply a by-product of leadership that knows how to get the most out of a team that is very talented. Thus, for me the highest standard is success—the knowledge that you have made the effort to teach your team how to work together at their highest level.

And that, in my opinion, is the first goal of leadership—namely, getting the very best out of the people in your organization, whether they have talent to spare or are spare on talent.

Let go of the blame. Reject the excuse that "If I only had more talented people, I could make this place great." Instead, embrace the question, "How can I lead my school (or my system) to greatness using the team that I have?" Most people do not show up to work in schools and school systems thinking *I'd like to just be mediocre today.* Most people want to learn, grow, and thrive. Every person on your crew has knowledge, gifts, and talents to share. Individually and collectively, they have the capacity to do amazing work. And as Coach Wooden noted above, it is a critical (and we believe FUN) part of your job as a leader to help bring out the best in your people.

Is it easy? No. In fact, discovering what's special about each person on your team takes time and focused energy. Do it anyway. Be relentless in seeking out and nurturing each person's greatness. Spend time with people, ask questions, watch them doing their jobs. Pay attention to what energizes them and publicly notice the impact they make. Tell them often how much you appreciate and value their unique contributions and how what they do helps the team and the school as a whole.

Be relentless in seeking out and nurturing each person's greatness.

Our days and weeks can be so jam-packed with "stuff" that it is easy to get overwhelmed with the sheer number of tasks on the to-do list. Investing every minute of our time in low-value tasks at the sacrifice of investing time in our people dooms us to walk the plank of mediocrity.

When we invest the time in getting to know the unique knowledge, skills, talents, and gifts that each person possesses, we not only build relationships and trust, but we also begin to build the knowledge we need as leaders—the knowledge to help us utilize and maximize the talents of our team in the best way possible. This then helps us move the entire team and school forward with a jolt of positive momentum.

WE ARE ON THE SAME TEAM CHALLENGE

- Reflect: Do you ever play the "blame game"?

- If you have been focused on placing blame on someone, stop and ask yourself: How can I reframe those thoughts in a more positive way?

- When you find yourself in a situation with colleagues who start to play the blame game, make a deliberate choice not to engage. Better yet, redirect the conversation in a more positive and fruitful direction.

- What do you see when you look at your team members? Instead of looking for flaws and faults, make a list of things you appreciate about your staff. Then, send a note of thanks or encouragement or, better yet, publicly acknowledge the good you see in the educators and administrative staff with whom you work.

 Share your thoughts, ideas, and artifacts with the *Lead Like a PIRATE* community using the #LeadLAP hashtag.

HARNESS THE
POWER OF TEAMS

*Leaders become great, not because of their power, but because
of their ability to empower others.*
—John Maxwell, *The 5 Levels of Leadership*

arly on in my career, I (Shelley) had been highly impacted by
Rick DuFour's work on Professional Learning Communities,
and I knew going into my first principalship that I wanted
impactful teams in place at my school—teams that knew they were
empowered to make decisions about teaching and learning. One of the
first teams we built at our school was the Site Leadership Team, which
was composed of one member of every grade-level team, our reading
specialist, resource teacher, and a special-education representative. To be
completely honest, building this team was not easy. I had some grade
levels where no one wanted to volunteer to join. I had to work really hard
to sell it, and in the end, I had a handful of people on the team, some
of whom had reluctantly agreed to give this team thing a shot, but they
weren't making any promises to stay.

One of the first things I did was take this team with me to a three-day professional-development institute where we learned from some of the leading educational experts in our field. After our three days at the institute, we had our own leadership team on-site meeting where I asked one question of the group: "Based on where we are as a school and the three days of learning we just had, what do you think we should do next?"

One of the teachers responded with, "Well, what do *you* think we should do?"

My answer helped cement in their minds my commitment to the team collectively and my belief in them individually. "I've read their books and studied their work, but I don't know that my thoughts carry any more weight than yours," I said. "We have all just been through three days of the same powerful learning experience together, and all three days we've discussed that it's really good stuff. You have all been at this school for a lot longer than I have. You know your colleagues, the students, the community better than I do. So I'd really like to hear what you think. Who would like to start?"

I was a new principal, the "new boss." They were still getting to know me, and I'm guessing that if I had said, "Here's what I think we should do . . ." the discussion would have stopped there. They didn't know me well enough at that point to know whether they could question or challenge what I said without risking their jobs. They didn't really know yet whether I would truly value their ideas or if I had just put this team together to "rubber stamp" my ideas. With all that in mind, there was *no way* I was going to speak first. In fact, I was determined to be the one to talk last, and I saw my role as one of summarizer and synthesizer of their collective thoughts and ideas. I asked a lot of clarifying questions that day and pushed people to say more. I asked them to evaluate their ideas in regard to our collective learning, asked what we needed to learn more about, categorized our collective thinking, asked about pros and cons, and mediated disagreements when necessary. And, eventually, I added my own thoughts and ideas to the discussion. But this was their school before it was mine, and their individual ideas and collective voice

Ten Tips for Teams That Tick

1. Start with a purpose! What is your team's mission? This is not just a fancy phrase to put at the top of your agendas; it is the nitty-gritty of what you're all about. Purpose = Action!

2. Develop shared norms and a respectful way to address when they are not followed.

3. Start each meeting with celebrations. This helps build the much-needed trust it takes for teams to function at high levels.

4. Agendas: Have them, follow them, have team members contribute.

5. Share the wealth! Take turns with different team roles to ensure shared leadership. Some of our favorites: facilitator, note taker, timekeeper, norm reader—what other roles can you come up with?

6. Sometimes teams need a timeout to vent. When done productively and professionally, taking a short, two-minute break to clear the air can make the remaining time more productive.

7. Share the minutes from your meeting with those in the group and any others in your organization who could benefit. Transparency bolsters trust and helps build a positive culture!

8. Use structures and protocols to be sure each team member has a chance to contribute. Sometimes the quietest ideas are the best for the team.

9. Invite a colleague who isn't on your team to observe your team meeting and give feedback on ways it can run more effectively.

10. Take time to review the action steps needed before the next meeting. When everyone knows the "to-do list," it helps the team to be productive and efficient.

Bonus Tip: At the end of your meeting, take time to evaluate how well your team stuck to norms and followed the agenda. Recalibrate for the next meeting and begin to set your new agenda.

mattered. It didn't make any sense for me to create a plan in isolation. I wanted a plan that would work for our school. To create that, I needed them.

What happened over the course of that day, I believe, was the first real turning point for our school. We set specific goals and established the first steps of an action plan that the team was committed to help move forward. Every person on the team had been given a voice and multiple opportunities to contribute. We ended our day by making commitments to each other, creating a plan for how our colleagues who weren't in the room with us could also have a voice, and we outlined what we needed to learn next. They left the meeting knowing they had done good work—work that they were proud and excited to share with the rest of our staff. We met several times during the course of that first year to refine our plan, identify obstacles, work through challenges, rethink next steps. We also read and learned together so we could improve our thinking and make wise decisions. While there were many indications throughout the year that this team was committed to the work and to making a significant impact, my proudest moment came during our last meeting of the year when one of the teachers thanked everyone for their commitment and hard work, then asked everyone on the team to commit to stay on the team for a second year—and they all agreed.

By my second year as a principal, our School Leadership Team was in full swing, and our Grade-Level Professional Learning Communities were up and running. We had additional leadership teams in place across the school tackling specific areas of need, including a team charged with helping us rethink our plan supporting the English Language Learners that comprised more than 60 percent of our student population, and another team that was evaluating and reworking our student-discipline plan and policies. Each one of these teams made a significant, positive impact on our school.

Over the course of our tenure as leaders in a variety of roles, we have embraced the power of teams, and we strategically create and empower teams to help design, implement, and monitor the work that needs to be done in our schools.

We treasure our teams. We believe in our teams. And our teams do great work.

But creating, accessing, and utilizing teams to help successfully lead the work in our schools can be a scary prospect for some leaders.

We treasure our teams. We believe in our teams. And our teams do great work.

During my (Shelley's) second year as a principal, one of my colleagues, someone I held in high regard and who had served many years as a beloved principal, wanted to chat with me after a principals' meeting about the teams we had built at our school. I was honored she had asked and was thrilled to talk with her—I can talk teaching, learning, and leadership all day long! We shared many ideas back and forth about teams, how to build them, what decisions should be decisions of a team vs. the decision of the principal, etc. And then she asked me the question:

"What happens if you turn a decision over to a team and they make the wrong decision?"

Her fear of that happening was very real, and to be honest, I'm not sure I answered her question very well because it was really the first time I had considered it.

At the core of that question is the concept of giving trust, which we discussed in Section I. There is never a guarantee that a team will make the exact same decision you might have, but if you empower and trust a team to make a decision, you have to let them take action. If you have already made up your mind about something and aren't willing to go in a different direction, then it's not a decision you should turn over to a team.

Another critical aspect to consider is what the parameters are for your teams when they come together to make decisions. Do you turn over a problem to solve, shout "Go!" and leave it to the loudest voice or strongest opinion to take over the group and bully people into going her way? We hope not, because that's a surefire way to lead your team to failure. While Beth and I believe wholeheartedly in working through teams to make decisions that help move the school or district forward, we also define specific parameters and guidelines within which we expect teams to work.

1. Never turn a decision that you have already made over to a team and then hope they choose the same thing. If you simply want the team to be a rubber stamp, don't create the team. It's okay for you to make a decision on your own as a leader. But if you charge the team with making the decision, trust them to make it!

2. When you build a team, be clear up front about whether it is an advisory team that will make recommendations or a decision-making team.

3. Make sure the goals of the team are clear and establish reasonable timelines to complete them.

4. As the school or district leader, be clear about your parameters within which they need to work. Being clear about what you can and cannot live with helps you avoid the situation of a team spending time tackling a challenge and making a decision and then you having to say "no." As a simple example, early on as a principal, I (Shelley) had a team who wanted to revise our school uniform policies. I told them upfront that:

    a. I did not have a preference one way or another about uniforms. I was fine if we had them but also fine if we didn't.

    b. I would never allow a child to be sent home from school to change because they were wearing the wrong clothes. My commitment to kids being in school learning would always trump wearing the right color shirt!

    c. Being "out of uniform" could not constitute a discipline referral to the office.

Setting these parameters from the beginning helped ensure the team did not create a plan which I could not ultimately support.

5. Purposely build your team from the onset with people who bring unique voices and diversity of thought to the table. Too often we leave people off our teams who we think of as negative or "resistant to change." Sometimes the reason they are resistant is simply because we never ask them to be a part of the process. We don't allow their voice to be heard until after a decision has been made and a plan is in place to carry it out.

6. Have clear ground rules and norms about how the group interacts with each other and works together so all voices are equally heard and valued.

7. Create an environment where challenging one another's ideas is welcomed and valued, but where attacking people is not.

8. Create shared learning experiences for the team. Decisions need to be based on evidence, research, learning, and not opinions. Continue to ask, "What do we need to learn more about? What additional data do we need to make a sound and wise decision?" Make it clear from the beginning that the team will need to share all data, information, research, evidence, etc. that helped shape their decision and plan. Typically, if we see a "bad decision" come out of a team, it's because the team was allowed to make a decision based on opinions, and the loudest voices won.

9. Commit to a plan, not perfection. It's okay if the initial plan doesn't work perfectly. Reflection, feedback, and revision need to be expected and valued parts of the process.

10. Provide authentic feedback to your team, help get obstacles out of their way, and appreciate their hard work and accomplishments.

11. Have a well-defined understanding of what "consensus" means and a process for reaching it.

12. Have a communication plan and a plan for those impacted by the team's decision to have some voice and choice within the decision.

Effective teams can elevate good schools and districts to great ones. As leaders, we need to model what we expect in teams, help set up conditions for success, and—sometimes—just get out of the way and let the magic happen! Teamwork isn't always perfect, and that's okay! We must be available to support teams, but avoid the urge to swoop in to "fix" issues. Just like in the classroom, some of the most powerful learning occurs through the right amount of struggle.

TEAM CHALLENGE

- What teams do you currently have in place in your school or district? Is there a clear, shared purpose for each team? Could each member of your staff quickly state this to a visitor to your school? How could this be a reality in your school?

- Reread Ten Tips for Teams that Tick (page 87). How could you apply these to your teams?

- How are decisions made at your school? How might you take ideas from this section to leverage shared leadership and decision making?

 Share your thoughts, ideas, and artifacts with the *Lead Like a PIRATE* community using the #LeadLAP hashtag.

Find the Magic in the People– the People– Not Programs

Magic is believing in yourself; if you can do that, you can make anything happen.
—Johann Wolfgang von Goethe

Of course there must be lots of Magic in the world," he said wisely one day, "but people don't know what it is like or how to make it. Perhaps the beginning is just to say nice things are going to happen until you make them happen. I am going to try and experiment.
—Frances Hodgson Burnett, *The Secret Garden*

And above all, watch with glittering eyes the whole world around you because the greatest secrets are always hidden in the most unlikely places. Those who don't believe in magic will never find it.
—Roald Dahl, *The Minpins*

We are sure that most of you, as we do, get an onslaught of daily emails and phone calls from publishing company sales reps trying to convince you that they have created the magic program that will provide answers to the challenges you face in ensuring all your students are successful learners. The sales reps have learned all the buzzwords. They will try to convince you they have the most engaging complex texts aligned perfectly to the standards you are trying to teach. Or they might be trying to convince you to buy the English-language-development program so flawlessly scripted that any adult in the building, regardless of grade or department, could teach it. They are certain they have created the perfect formula for building strong, conceptual understanding of fractions for every third grader in your building.

In addition to the sales reps, you probably also have educators in your school or system who try to convince you that if they just had a better program, a better script to follow, a Teacher's Edition with end-less worksheets, their lives would be easier and their students would be learning more.

While we certainly want to put the most amazing resources in the hands of our teachers, we are even more committed to developing amaz-ing teachers. Programs don't teach kids; teachers do, and teachers are capable of making magic happen for kids. The solution to any school challenge or issue is never just a new program. It is a commitment to the people who are doing the work. It is building a sense of self-efficacy in the individuals on your team and convincing them that the magic isn't in the latest initiative or curriculum mandate—the magic is in them.

Programs don't teach kids; teachers do, and teachers are capable of making magic happen for kids.

So if success isn't the result of the latest and greatest program, how do we reach it? What do we do instead? We invest in our people. States, districts, and schools across the country spend millions of dollars on pro-grams while at the same time slashing budgets for professional develop-ment and learning. We think that is a mistake. We do everything within our control to make sure we build in as much time as we can for personal learning and growth. We make professional learning a top priority. We harness every available minute and spend every dollar we can on building the capacity of the people who are being asked to teach and guide the next generation.

Then, we take what we've learned, roll up our sleeves, and start doing the work alongside our staff and teachers. We make mistakes, and we learn from them. Our teachers make mistakes, and we don't beat them up; rather, we appreciate them for going on the journey, and we give them feedback to help push their learning to the next level. We build in time for individual and collective reflection, and we make adjustments as we go. We laugh and we cry, we congratulate and we console, and we push each other to be better tomorrow than we were today.

During my (Shelley's) first year as principal, our district had just adopted a new reading program. The mandate at the time was "fidelity to the core." (That phrase seriously still causes me to break out in hives!) I recall being completely taken aback when, during my interview for the position, someone asked how I would hold teachers accountable to following the program exactly as written. The concept of cookie-cutter teaching goes against everything I believe in, but I must have come up with a good-enough answer because I got the job. In my first couple of months, I spent time in classrooms observing lessons. While some of them were just fine, I saw several examples of teachers reading instructions from textbooks and off of worksheets. I even heard a teacher apologizing to a student with an, "I'm sorry, I don't know what it means; but we still have to try to do something to answer question number three."

Teachers were deflated, students weren't learning any more than they were before, and I was heartbroken. Frustrated with the ineffective mandates, I launched a campaign with my staff. I wanted them to know that the program was not going to define us. Instead, we were going to define how the program could benefit us and support what we knew to be in the best interests of students. I gave my staff permission to break free from the textbooks. I made a clear statement: I believe in YOU, and together we are going to create the educational experiences we know our students need.

We started on a journey of examining data, engaging in professional learning about reading and, collectively, we defined what our instructional program should be for reading/language arts. We ended up using the program as our primary resource, but we were no longer chained to it. We threw out the pieces we didn't find valuable, and we incorporated other resources to help fill in the gaps. Ultimately, we created a program we were proud of and it was ours.

At the end of my first year as principal, we admittedly still had abysmal test scores. They had actually even gone down a bit from the year before, but I had built solid relationships, and we had worked really hard and created a powerful plan to move forward the following year. Student learning increased significantly; we had the test scores to validate that, but even more importantly, we also had our own internal observations and personal stories from students and parents. We had writing samples and student read-alouds and students who were much more engaged in their own learning. Our teachers were more invested, and beginning that next year our test scores (which were definitely important for my job security) were on the rise.

Teaching is incredibly complex! It involves classroom management, engagement techniques, depth of content knowledge, precise use of effective instructional practices, wise use of resources, an understanding of assessment and how to use it, long-term planning and short-term adjustments. It involves knowing the unique learning needs of each child in the classroom and developing strategies to reach them and help them thrive. It involves grit, determination, persistence, flexibility, an element of fun, and a whole lot of heart! No program has that kind of magic, but teachers do. Believe in them, invest in them, build in time for learning and growth, and watch the magic happen.

People, Not Programs Challenge

- How can you convey to your staff that the magic lies within them, rather than within the program?

- How can you clearly communicate to your staff that programs are resources to support them rather than resources that define and confine them?

- Take a closer look at the programs you have implemented in your school. Have you left room for professional judgment in their implementation?

- Do teachers in your building feel constrained by the programs in your system, or do they have some freedom to innovate and create powerful learning experiences for kids?

- How can you more clearly communicate to your staff that you honor and support their personal creativity and innovation?

Share your thoughts, ideas, and artifacts with the *Lead Like a PIRATE* community using the #LeadLAP hashtag.

GET THE RIGHT
PEOPLE ON THE SHIP

A crowd is a tribe without a leader. A crowd is a tribe without communication. Most organizations spend their time marketing to the crowd. Smart organizations assemble the tribe.
—Seth Godin, *Tribes*

PIRATE leaders can't do it alone. As Dave says in *Teach Like a PIRATE*, "All pirates travel with a crew; you can't sail, navigate, and fight battles all on your own." Your crew is essential to the survival of your building and the success of your students. Having the right people on board doing the right things is in everyone's best interest.

Sometimes you get to pick your crew; other times they are on board when you get there. Either way, in order to keep your ship afloat and, more importantly, keep your ship moving in the right direction, you need to make your mission and intentions clear from the moment you come aboard. Everyone must know where you are heading and, if possible, be part of setting the course. You must look at each staff opening you have as an opportunity for your own growth and that of the school. Look for people who bring something needed to your crew. And remember: You can never have too much passion.

We want people who can motivate our current crew to strive for greatness.

The interview process is a prime opportunity for adding the right people to your crew. Take time to carefully craft that process. What are the typical questions you ask? Are they laden with buzzwords and candidate definitions? After introductions, I (Beth) ask the applicant to tell me about a lesson they have taught that they could have sold tickets to. I absolutely love to see the looks on their faces. This question is like no other they've ever been asked. From the way that they handle this question, I can immediately tell if they are a good fit for our crew. The amount of reflection that goes into this question shows me if a teacher is willing and passionate enough to make an impact in our school. Bland lessons are not what we are looking for. Most anyone can learn the curriculum standards. We want more than that. We want people who can take those standards and turn them into magic for our students. We want people who can motivate our current crew to strive for greatness. We need an energy from the candidate that will support the existing passions and inspire new passions amongst those already here.

After the ticket question, we move into other questions regarding our building practices. Anyone can tell me the meaning of a PLC, but what I really want to know is your beliefs and action regarding collaborative culture, how learning and assessment are related, what you do when students don't understand concepts, and what you do when they already know how to do something. I don't want to know your philosophy on behavior management. I want to give you a scenario from one of our real-life classrooms and hear how you would handle the situation. And then I'll push you a little and ask you to tell me what you would then do if your first solution didn't work, and then what you would do if you still weren't successful. These questions aren't meant to frustrate or cause more

Sample Interview Questions

1. Convince me that I should place my own child in your classroom.

2. Describe for us a lesson you could sell tickets to.

3. What is something you have read lately that has impacted you deeply as an educator?

4. What is the toughest situation you have faced as an educator and how have you handled it?

5. What would you do between now and the beginning of the year to prepare for your new position?

6. If you were to write a book for other educators, what would be the title?

7. What makes a stellar school? Teammate? Administrator?

8. You have just walked out of a classroom and said, "Wow! That was an amazing learning experience for students!" What did you see?

9. Greatness is a moving target. How do you keep moving toward greatness?

10. What are you passionate about? How do you showcase your passions in your position?

11. How could you use social media to tell the story of your classroom?

12. What do you do to connect and collaborate with educators outside your system?

13. Beyond the mandated professional development in your school/district, what do you do to continue your growth as an educator?

14. Tell me about a lesson that failed and what you did next.

15. At the end of the school year, what five words would you hope your students would use to describe your classroom?

Bonus: Ask your interview team what they most want in a new crew member. Challenge them to craft a question or two that reflects those passions.

anxiety, but they are designed to reveal the people who have what it takes to join our crew. I want to see the sparkle of resiliency and the gumption of a risk taker. I want to see their passion for learning come to life in the answers they share. I want to know before they leave that they are willing to revise, redo, change, take risks, fail forward, and do whatever it takes to help our students succeed. Because those are the people who have the character, knowledge, and skill to help us live out our mission of becoming the best middle school ever.

Finally, I always close interviews with a simple question that reveals so much: "What is something you've read lately that has influenced you as an educator?" Their answer tells the interview panel if our prospective crew member is truly a lifelong learner. It also lets us know if their beliefs and practices are aligned to our mission, vision, and collective commitments. The answer reveals whether the potential pirate really walks the talk.

Finding the Crew Challenge

- Take a look at the current interview questions you or your school district asks. Do these questions align with your mission and vision? Do they help to set apart the good from the great? How do the candidates show—not just tell—the philosophies and practices that they could bring to your school?

- Take time in a staff meeting to brainstorm "traditional" interview questions. Work together to PIRATE up those questions to align to the type of teacher you want on your ship.

 Share your thoughts, ideas, and artifacts with the *Lead Like a PIRATE* community using the #LeadLAP hashtag.

If It's Important ...
Make Time for It.

Lack of direction, not lack of time, is the problem. We all have twenty-four-hour days.
—Zig Ziglar

Time is a created thing. To say, "I don't have time," is like saying "I don't want to."
—Lao Tzu

If you ask any educator what they need more of, almost all of them will say, "time." It is a commodity more precious to us than money. There are never enough hours in the day and our jobs are never done. The phrase "what gets monitored gets done," is a common refrain in our field. We offer this simple alternative: "What you make time for gets done."

One of the biggest mistakes leaders can make is to set goals and priorities for the school or district, and then just tell people to go and do them. This happens every year (every day!) in education, and it isn't long before administrators start scratching their heads wondering why teachers aren't doing what was expected of them.

If something is truly a priority, you have to make time for it. And if you're a leader, you can't just make time for yourself; you have to make sure your teachers and staff have the time they need to work on that priority. So, if you want your school to be a learning organization, build in time for learning. If you want your teachers to collaborate, build collaboration time into your schedules. If you want to implement a new reading initiative, build in cycles of learning, practice, reflection, feedback, and revision.

One of the most important exercises I (Shelley) did for myself each year as a principal was to total up the number of hours teachers actually had outside of their classrooms to do something other than the actual work of teaching. (As an assistant superintendent, I did something similar with the number of hours principals had outside of their schools.) I looked at the hours they had before school and after school according to their contracts, the hours recaptured for minimum days, the number of hours teachers were back at work the week before students started school, etc. I counted every hour available outside classroom-teaching time. The total varied from year to year a bit, but it usually landed somewhere around 213 hours. About 135 of those hours consisted of the 30 minutes a teacher had in their contract before school started and the 15 minutes in their contract after school was out for students. In general those hours were allocated for individual teacher prep. That left about 78 hours of time that teachers were contracted to be on campus outside of their teaching time. Deduct at least eight of those hours for teachers to have some time on their own in their classrooms on at least one of those pre-school days, and that number drops down to 70 hours of time that we had left for teachers to do something other than teach. *Seventy hours.* That is less than two weeks. If there are even three new things on your list that you are asking teachers to accomplish in a given year, each one gets about twenty-three hours of time *if* you maximize all the time you have to support those changes and initiatives. No wonder people feel overwhelmed!

One of the best things this exercise did for me was to encourage focus. It helps me answer the question: "What is *the* most important work we have to accomplish together this year?" Once I have identified that most important work, it helps me protect every minute of those seventy hours from distractions. It helps me say "no!" to the flashy, "flavor of the month" ideas and initiatives that can come along and can so easily turn our attention to things that are less important.

The other thing this exercise did was force me to allocate resources to finding more time to accomplish our goals. One of the first (and easiest) things I did (both as a principal and assistant superintendent) was ditch traditional staff meetings that consisted of a laundry list of "to-dos" and informational items. If the information could be shared in writing, it went out to everyone in a weekly update. Our time together was too precious to spend it reading things people could read for themselves. That simple change allowed our time together to focus on learning, planning, sharing, and reflecting on our top priorities.

When you examine the real number of hours you have to work with, it forces you to confront the question: "Is that enough time?" If the answer is "no," you have an obligation to figure out ways to get more time—for yourself and for your crew. Another example from my principal years was reallocating funds to literally buy ourselves ninety minutes per week within the school day for grade-level teams to collaborate. We used some of our budget to pay for part-time teachers to teach our students art, physical education, and fun components of science (all things teachers were struggling to work into their days).

If you have an initiative or a project you want to accomplish, it isn't enough to tell people what to do.

Time is both valuable and scarce! If you have an initiative or a project you want to accomplish, it isn't enough to tell people what to do. You must also show them why it is important enough to devote time to—and you must show them how they can fit it into their schedules. That may mean you need to reexamine what everyone is doing and eliminate old, low-impact practices to create time for more productive practices.

TIME CHALLENGE

- Reflect: If you were starting a new school from scratch, would you implement all of the curriculum, practices, policies, etc. that are in place at your school now? If the answer is "no," how might you eliminate those things from your school?

- People will generally invest time in what matters. Take a serious look at your school's curriculum and activities. Make sure everything has a purpose and that you don't promote doing something simply because "We've always done that!" What things could go? What things are worth keeping?

- Count *your* hours! How many hours do you honestly have with your team to work on new initiatives? Is it enough for all the ones you are trying to lead? If not, what can you take off your plate?

 Share your thoughts, ideas, and artifacts with the *Lead Like a PIRATE* community using the #LeadLAP hashtag.

Make Changes
without Capsizing
Your Ship

*The only limit to your impact is your imagination
and commitment.*
—Anthony Robbins

You believe in your people. You've decided to invest in them. You've built your teams and empowered them to do great work. You've narrowed down your priorities and evaluated the time you have and allocated more time if you needed it, and now you're ready to go! You know you want to move forward, make a change, or lead a new initiative. So what now? What are some of the other things you need to consider?

Be a learner of what it means to lead complex change. Change is a process, not a one-time event. To lead change, you must anticipate and understand how change impacts people, and that means being strategic as you plan for change. Get clear about the expectations you have for the change, then carefully consider the systems of support you will need to provide for people as you ask them to do some of their work differently.

Understand that "full implementation" of anything takes time and does not happen in a single year. While I (Shelley) was an assistant superintendent, our district made the transition to full implementation of the Common Core State Standards. But it didn't happen all at once. In year one, what full implementation really meant was that we all agreed to make the switch from one set of standards to another, and we agreed we would begin to grapple with them on a daily basis. We had worked with teacher and administrator teams to develop a framework for new units of study aligned to the CCSS. So "full implementation" in year one meant that we were all going to use these units as the foundation for our work.

Our commitment to implementing this new set of standards led us to ask and answer the question: "What will be different in our schools and classrooms next year as a result of our Common Core alignment and implementation?"

To successfully make any significant change, you must have clearly articulated goals about the implementation. You also need standards of measurement so you know if you are getting better and closer to reaching your goals. And at the end of the year, it is essential to evaluate where you have been, celebrate how far you've come, and define your next steps.

Choose a starting point and get really good at it. Continuing with the Common Core example, while all of the Common Core Standards for ELA were in play for us our first year, there were many things we needed to learn in order for us to be truly aligned to the Common Core expectations. It wasn't enough to know about them, we really needed to know them. We asked schools to choose one or two of these areas of focus (remember how few hours they actually have to do this work together; there is not time enough to do it all!), learn deeply, and work together to infuse those practices into classrooms across the school and get good at them. Some schools started by deepening their understanding of close reading and text complexity while others started with deepening their learning around the Webb's Depth of Knowledge framework and using it to design higher-level tasks aligned to the standards. With any new initiative, there are often several entry points for us to begin the work; let people choose their path.

Foster an environment of collaboration and learning. When you introduce a new initiative at either the school or district level, you are asking all of the educators in your system to make changes and do things differently. In order to be successful, it's critical to create time for learning and collaboration. It's essential to build as much of it as you can into the schedule and not expect that everyone learns it all on their own.

Learning about what we don't understand helps reduce anxiety, as does having colleagues and partners with whom we can work through challenges and celebrate successes. Learning and collaboration also make us better.

Employees crave clarity; they want to know precisely what they can do to be most effective—and then not be distracted from that. The highest priorities—the core—must be clarified incessantly. Clarity is the antidote to anxiety ... if you do nothing else as a leader, be clear.

—Marcus Buckingham, *The One Thing You Need to Know*

Part of learning is taking risks and trying things differently. Understand that when you (or your staff members) try something new, you won't always be good at it the first time you do it. Trial and error is part of the learning process, so celebrate approximations, offer feedback, and provide additional learning and practice time. Expect and allow for mistakes. It's all part of learning.

Understand the big picture and focus on the good of the initiative. Sometimes it is hard to get on board with a new initiative or change. And the reality is that no new initiative is perfect and no change occurs without mishaps. Lucy Calkins, Mary Ehrenworth, and Chris Lehman pose this question in the first chapter of their book, *Pathways to the Common Core*: "Will you choose to view the Common Core Standards as curmudgeons or as if they are gold?" Replace "Common Core Standards" with whatever your new initiative is and the question works. If you understand and talk about what's at the heart of the change, you may be able to build more commitment to the shifts. It's hard to create passion for a program, but you can create enthusiasm and build commitment around great ideas.

Be deliberate about making connections to work you are already doing. When my (Shelley's) district made the transition to the Common Core, we already had a strong literacy initiative in place in our schools, and there were several practices that were in alignment with Common Core goals. A new initiative isn't always about everything being brand-new. Often it is about enhancing and refining work you have already started, but making the connections is critical. To make those connections, ask, "How does what we are already doing align with the new expectations?" and "What pieces do we still need to strengthen or add?"

It is important to understand how the new initiative is **different *from what you are already doing.*** While it is critical to make connections to current work, it's just as essential to be crystal clear about what's different and the implications those differences have for teaching and learning. Be honest about what the differences are; you don't want to send the message that this is the same old thing with a new label. Deliberately define what's different and give people a vision for what the new initiative might look like in the classroom. When Common Core was introduced, some teachers took it as an invitation to dust off the old dinosaur unit from fifteen years ago. They didn't have the depth of understanding of what Common Core required. It's the leader's job to work alongside teachers to identify what's different and how it connects (or doesn't connect) to current and even past practices.

Change for change's sake or change without a really good reason behind it will get you nowhere.

Know and share your "why" but be prepared for the "here's why not." Simon Sinek says in his book, *Start with Why*, "People don't buy what you do; they buy why you do it." Sinek's work has had a big impact on many of us in education. We make reference to the fact that we need to start and share the "why" as a way for us to help build commitment to the new initiative or the new work. And it's true: Change for change's sake or change without a really good reason behind it will get you nowhere.

While it's important to convey and share the why, it's equally important to be ready to respond to the folks who exclaim, "Here's why not!" Part of successfully building commitment to something new is being prepared for what the obstacles will be and where resistance might come from. Before you propose a change, come up with a plan to address the pushback. Knowing the objections individuals or teams might have and addressing them from the beginning helps break down the barriers of defensiveness some people might have initially to a change. The more barriers you can break down from the beginning, the more open people are to listening and considering the change. If you know the new change is going to add something to people's plates, be prepared to take something else off. If you know there will be a big learning curve for people, share the professional learning plan and a timeline that allows for professional learning, practice, coaching, feedback, and reflective dialogue.

If you want to build commitment to something new, you must be fully aware of the impact the change will have on people. Celebrate the positive changes, for sure, but also be fully prepared to support people through what they perceive to be the negative impacts of the change.

Avoid the deer-in-the-headlights looks. I (Shelley) once had someone who worked for me who later moved into a principal role. She often sought out my advice as she started in her position, and one of the things she asked me was, "How did you avoid the 'deer-in-the-headlights' looks at staff meetings when you introduced a new initiative, a new task, or any kind of change?" It was a great question, and caused me some pause, but ultimately my answer to her was that by the time I had something on a staff meeting agenda for the whole group to discuss, I wasn't really taking anyone by surprise.

Change isn't something you just announce from the podium at a staff meeting. Change builds over time as people get used to the idea of doing something different. If you want to implement something new and make it amazing, put in the time and build the foundation for several weeks or even months before putting it before the whole team and committing to the change. Visit with and share some of the ideas with grade-level teams, departments, or any other small team that might be impacted. Get their advice and thoughts. Stop by the classrooms of those you initially think might be opposed to the new idea or initiative and engage them in conversations and seek their guidance. Ask them what obstacles and challenges they might foresee, how the change might impact them, what support they think people might need if it's going to be a success. Then use that information to tweak and revise the plan. Share the new ideas with established small groups and teams, ask for their feedback and thoughts, then use it!

By the time a new initiative or big change makes it onto a staff meeting agenda for discussion and possible implementation, people shouldn't be surprised. They should have already had opportunities to discuss it with you. They've been able to share their hopes and their fears and the types of things they might need to support them, and they see those things represented and addressed in the plan you present. They each, in their own way, have made contributions to the idea over time and hopefully can see a little bit of themselves in the new initiative you propose and the plan you have to support them in making it happen.

> *Change is an opportunity to do something amazing.*
> —George Couros, *The Innovator's Mindset*

Change, no matter how big or little, can be stressful. As the leader, you must have a depth of understanding about the change and then introduce it to your staff in small bites while making sure they understand the importance of the changes. Like teaching, you want to scaffold the learning for your staff until they are able to have a complete understanding of the initiative. Everyone is watching you; you must lead the change in a positive and specific way in order for it to be effective and long lasting.

NAVIGATE CHANGE CHALLENGE

- What needs to change in your organization so that it can make a more significant impact on the students' learning experience?

- How does that change support your overall mission? How will you explain that connection to your crew?

- What deliberate steps can you take to be proactive, build the foundation, and avoid the "deer--in-the-headlights" syndrome?

- When you are charged with leading a new program or initiative, what steps do you take to deepen your own learning? Commit to taking a deep dive alongside your team to truly understand the work.

Share your thoughts, ideas, and artifacts with the *Lead Like a PIRATE* community using the #LeadLAP hashtag.

Use Stories to Personalize Data

A story is a way to say something that can't be said any other way.
—Flannery O'Connor, *Mystery and Manners*

Crickets. After spending hours and hours sifting through mountains of data, working to understand the implications, and creating pages and pages of colorful tables, charts, and graphs to share in fancy presentations to your team, you're expecting, well, something. You hope people will *ooh* and *ahh* at the hours of work you have put into making sense of the data. You pray that presenting it in a meaningful way will convince people to make a change and to do things differently. Instead, you hear crickets, or, worse, your presentation brings on snickers and yawns.

The reality is that, oftentimes, the numbers, test scores, and standardized data you work so hard to understand as a leader seems boring or unimportant to the people on your team. Just like a teaching hook captures student interest, painting a picture through a collection of stories that capture people's hearts is much more effective at initiating change than sharing pages and pages of data charts.

Painting a picture through stories that capture people's hearts is much more effective at initiating change than sharing pages and pages of data charts.

Early on in my (Shelley's) principalship, I knew we needed to make big changes to the work we were doing to support our English learners. I set out to convince people of this desperate need by using almost an entire ninety-minute staff meeting to share all the data I could find. I spent hours putting together the data, and I delivered what I believed a very strong case for opening the dialogue about how to do things differently. Instead, I was met with several reasons justifying the data and excuses for why it wasn't better. You've heard them all:

"It takes four to seven years for language mastery."

"We have a high mobility rate; most of our kids are in and out and don't stick with us for the long haul."

"Lots of our English learners are also special ed."

"We have so many kids absent on so many days."

And, unique to our setting at the time, we had two sets of program options for English learners. Teachers in each program blamed the teachers of the other. I was stunned. Did they really not see what I was seeing? It was right there on the screen in red and green. How did they not feel the same sense of urgency that I did?

Upon reflection, I realized that while my team could clearly see that fewer than 10 percent of our English learners were scoring proficient or advanced on the standardized tests, they didn't *feel* it. So I tried another tactic at our next meeting. I sorted the data in a very different way. I just looked at sixth grade students from the year before, those English learners we had just sent on to middle school. There were seventy-three of them. I removed every child for which an excuse had been made. I took out the students who were also identified as having special needs. I took out every child who had not been in our school since kindergarten or first grade, and removed other students with inconsistent attendance. I was left with thirty-two students. About half of them had participated in the Bilingual program and the other half in the Sheltered English program, and only three of them scored proficient or advanced, two from the bilingual program and one from the Sheltered English program. These thirty-two kids were kids we owned, and three of them were performing at the level they should. These were kids whose stories we could tell, whose faces we could see, whose families we had known for at least six years. The impact this meeting had was the one I'd been hoping for; not only could they see the need, but they could feel it too. Those stories and the emotional connection they created were the jump-start we needed to begin talking about what needed to happen next.

Another example of how using stories can propel you forward came a bit later in my principalship. A challenge with our scheduling became evident through stories people were sharing with me. I knew we needed to make changes. As we are all aware, changing schedules can be a daunting task, perhaps second only in stress to grading and report cards. I am not sure why we hold practices like a 10:00 a.m. recess time so sacred, but we do.

So in an effort to begin the dialogue about our schedules, I opened our staff meeting with a handful of stories that had been shared with me. I told them about the sixth-grade teacher who had shared a frustration that, in a complete school day, she had her entire class in the room with her for only twenty minutes each day. I told the story of a conversation I'd had with a mom of a fifth grader who told me her high-school daughter had been teaching math to her fifth-grade sister. Why? Because she was pulled out every day for special-education services during the math time (and she only required special education support for reading). I told several others stories and afterward, I invited the staff to share their stories about how the schedule was impacting their students. When we finished, I asked, "So what should we do about it?" The dialogue that followed ultimately led us to a completely revamped schedule for the following school year.

STORY CHALLENGE

- Reflect: Think about the last initiative you proposed that fell on deaf ears—or was met with outright opposition. Did you include a personal narrative in your proposal? In other words, did you make it personal or tie an emotional connection to the request?

- When you turn numbers into names and facts into faces you make your message more powerful. How can you transform a message you want to deliver to your staff through the power of stories?

 Share your thoughts, ideas, and artifacts with the *Lead Like a PIRATE* community using the #LeadLAP hashtag.

Unleash Social Media to Tell Your School's Story

A hashtag is not just about communication, but developing community.
—George Couros, *The Innovator's Mindset*

The traditional ways we communicate with families and our communities—newsletters, emails, and school websites—do not engage them the same way an Instagram or Facebook post does. The high-connection factor of social media provides students, teachers, and even administrators with a power prior generations did not have at their disposal.
—Ryan McLane and Eric Lowe, *Your School Rocks . . . So Tell People!*

Most people form opinions about schools based on what they hear. There continues to be quite a bit of negative publicity around our schools. Much of this comes from a few bad things that happen or from someone who feels their child (or they) were wronged by a particular person in a school or the school itself. The problem is, no one is telling the real story of the amazing things that go on every day in our schools. It's up to us to insure that we transparently share what is going on in our buildings every day and to make sure our communities hear (and see) the real story. With the advent and power of social media, schools now have the tools to connect with the world and tell everyone what is really happening.

> *With social media, schools now have the tools to connect with the world and tell everyone what is really happening.*

Each year, McIntire Elementary strived to increase both parent and community involvement. Time conflicts for busy parents, teachers, and students meant that traditional PTO and evening events were not heavily attended. The school and PTO sent out surveys in an effort to get feedback about how to best involve parents and the community in school, but there was never a clear answer. The leadership team and I (Beth) knew it was time to rethink what parent and community involvement really meant for schools. Did involvement just mean coming into the school? Wasn't our real goal to engage our parents and the community with what was happening in our schools? Wasn't the point to create a culture of trust and rapport so that families who couldn't come to the building could still be involved? I knew that if we truly opened our schools so that everyone could be a part of the day-to-day operations, engagement at home would increase. But how could we realistically make that happen?

At that principal conference I attended in the summer of 2014, I had the opportunity to see how other schools across the country were doing the very thing that my team and I from McIntire strived to achieve. Through rethinking communication and engagement and using technology more effectively, parents and the community were brought into classrooms virtually each day. I was introduced to the work of Eric Sheninger's Digital Leadership, which laid the groundwork for how to successfully set up and implement school social-media sites to tell the story of your school and involve parents and the community. I also made connections to other principals who were doing amazing things to engage their families and communities. One principal had started doing snow-day read-alouds with his students that then continued into regular events. Another principal created video newsletters to reach out to those who may struggle with reading. I could not wait to get back to school to brainstorm with my staff and PTO to reshape what parent and community engagement could look like at McIntire Elementary.

As the summer continued, the first social-media adventure I embarked upon was an online read-aloud. First, I participated in one by new principal colleagues, Jay Billy and Chris Turnbull, held for their students in New Jersey. Then, during their next online read-aloud, I was invited to be a reader as well. The first cross-country principal read-aloud was amazing! These principals showcased their love of literacy in a fun way for students and parents alike. I then went solo and did a special read-aloud for upcoming kindergarteners getting ready to enter our school. It allowed me to begin to build important relationships with both the students and their parents—before school even began! It also started a buzz that something different was happening at McIntire Elementary. We created even more ways to connect, with a Twitter account for the school where I Tweeted out information and pictures of the building as the new school year approached. Not many parents in our town were on Twitter yet, so I also started a blog at principalhouf.blogspot.com and shared the link via email and Facebook to our parents.

I used the blog to replace the traditionally emailed/printed newsletter, and my first post offered back-to-school information that had previously been sent home in a mailing. The blog enabled visual aspects as well as an opportunity for two-way communication by posting and/or emailing. Our parents, students, and community members all were able to get a look into our school. (Teachers were also excited to see their hard work in classrooms showcased on the blog.) And unlike a traditional paper newsletter, the blog tracked analytics to see how many people had viewed it.

When the school year started, we polled parents about what forms of communication worked best for them. Email and Facebook were the overwhelming requests from parents. This feedback enabled our staff to rethink how we sent home information. I then started a school Facebook page. In one weekend, more than 200 parents had liked the page—some had even filled out a rating on the school. Emailing and posting newsletters, flyers, and other traditionally printed materials on social media became the new norm. (Some parents still requested paper copies and the school made sure to make this happen as well by keeping track of them in the office.) Through better forms of communication, the school was able to help parents be both involved and engaged in the success of our students.

Parents, family members from afar, and the community engaged with our daily Twitter posts about school happenings. Some commented, others sent me direct messages. The positive reviews for the school continued on Facebook. I also continued with the online read-alouds with students after school hours and later added these into the school day as well. Using Google Hangouts on Air (now YouTube Live), I was able to archive the read-alouds for access anytime. This became one more way to build positive relationships and helped instill a love for reading with our students and families while showcasing our literacy practices.

With the increased use of technology for communication, I worked with our staff and PTO to implement monthly family technology nights. These were held at McIntire, but were also shared electronically to families that were not able to attend. Each month, our lead technology teacher, Casey Echelmeier, and I provided learning for families and hands-on time to implement the strategies shared. Parents and grandparents attended and were grateful for assistance.

SHARING STORIES WITH SOCIAL MEDIA

Newsletter/Blog: bit.ly/Mc1stblog
Technology Night: bit.ly/McFamTN
Read-Aloud Archives: bit.ly/McReadAloud
Read-Aloud Videos: bit.ly/FMSHNYSs
Principal Introduction: bit.ly/meetmrshouf
Twitter How-To Module: bit.ly/HoufTwitter

We appreciated that feedback, as it was instrumental in preparing for and improving the next month's technology night.

Using social media wasn't really about the technology; it was about creating opportunities for engagement and involvement. These tools allowed parents and the community to better support learners because they knew what was going on in our school. The transparency and excitement for the day-to-day classroom events helped lead to better communication between the school and our families and, most importantly, between the students and their parents. Gone were the days of "we didn't do anything at school today." Also, the positive effect of increased communication and engagement led to an increased amount of family participation in activities held at school.

In the spring of 2015, I was asked to move to Fulton Middle School. Before the school year was over, I began using the same technology to engage my new school community. Working together with the technology teacher, Jan Bailey, we created a Facebook and Twitter account for Fulton Middle School. I also sent a parent newsletter through Smore. com. I began offering remote professional development to the teachers at FMS through Smore as well.

With the 2015–2016 school year underway, I used communication techniques similar to those I used at the elementary school to engage the families and staff at FMS. After listening to student feedback, I added Instagram to our tech toolbox. Online read-alouds were not as popular with middle schoolers, so I added videos to our newsletters. We also added videos to staff newsletters as we worked to find the most effective tool to communicate structures and expectations.

Your community wants to know what is happening in your school—and you need to be the one telling the story.

The buzz about shifts in communication began to spread across the district. The district professional-development team invited me to join them for a meeting to brainstorm ways to effectively use Twitter to build district-wide visibility, culture, and communication. A district hashtag was developed (#fpslearn) and used by the teaching staff to showcase the amazing things happening in schools across the district via Twitter. Immediately, all stakeholders had a glimpse into our district buildings and classrooms—from the comfort of their favorite digital device. The power of a common hashtag helped to build collaborative culture within buildings and throughout the district.

Since I started this journey of using social media to share and communicate with our school community, I've found a few resource gems that have helped with tips and ideas. *Your School Rocks!* by Ryan McLane and Eric Lowe offers ideas and strategies they use in their schools every day to better connect their families and communities. I especially love the examples of video newsletters that they have their students help create. Such amazing empowerment and ownership!

If you are new to the world of Twitter, never fear—*140 Twitter Tips for Educators* by Brad Currie, Billy Krakower, and Scott Rocco will have you Tweeting with the best of them in no time! The screenshots and practical tips have been wonderful when getting new teachers on Twitter.

Your community wants to know what you are about and what is happening in your school—and you need to be the one telling the story. Use communication methods that fit your community and the needs of your constituents. Be transparent and open your doors to the world through social media. Share the amazing things you see happening in your schools every day. Tell your story proudly and publicly—before someone else tells a different story.

TELL YOUR STORY CHALLENGE

- Reflect: How do you currently tell your school's story? Is it effective? What is the best tool or avenue for you to use to get your message out? How do you know?

- Use your favorite tool to create a brief survey of your families to find out their preferences on communication.

- Start a school or district hashtag and get your team involved.

- Engage your community actively by sharing the amazing work happening at your school and encouraging your teachers to do the same.

 Share your thoughts, ideas, and artifacts with the *Lead Like a PIRATE* community using the #LeadLAP hashtag.

Doing What's "Best" for Kids?

You've probably seen an image like the one below on social media:

The positive intent of this message is admirable. Meeting the needs of students should be the primary focus of what we do in our schools and districts. But this message can, unintentionally, be received in a way that damages school culture. Here's why:

The phrase "I'm going to do what's best for kids" can easily be interpreted by the receiver as "I don't believe you have the best interest of students in mind." And yes, there are times when the people making decisions do so solely in their own best interests. But those instances are pretty rare in education. Most educators we have worked with do typically make decisions based on the belief that they are doing what's best for kids.

Imagine this scenario: You, as the administrator, want to add an after-school-intervention program to the end of the school day for your third-grade students who are not reading at grade level—and you want your teachers to sign up to teach it. You propose the idea because of your conviction and commitment to the idea that it's best for kids to leave third grade as strong readers.

You have some teachers who agree with you and are in full support of the program, but you also have one third-grade teacher who tells you she refuses to have anything to do with it and, beyond that, she plans to discourage the parents from having their children attend. You and she argue about it, and you end the argument by telling the teacher that you are moving forward because you do "what's best for kids." She interprets your statement to mean that you do not believe she has her students' best interest at heart, and she leaves the conversation angry and feeling as if you don't value her work. Trust has eroded and this relationship has gone south.

What if we told you, though, that her perceived "unwillingness" to participate in and promote the after-school program did, in fact, come from her core belief that she is standing up for and doing what is best for kids. In her mind, her third-grade students have spent seven hours in school already. She runs small-group interventions throughout the day targeted to her students' needs and, while not at grade-level yet, they are making progress. She knows that several of her students are involved in sports, music, and other after-school activities, and she does not want to ask them to sacrifice these other activities for the extended reading program. She also believes that after a full day of school, students need some downtime so they can play and just be kids.

Who's to say which one of you is right? The reality is, a case could be made for both arguments being in the best interest of kids. Presuming you are doing what's best for kids while she (or anyone else on your staff) is not can be a quick way to create mistrust and dissolve culture.

Our challenge is this: As educational leaders, let's just presume that all of the educators we work with have the best interests of kids at heart. We may disagree from time to time on the methods or even the needs. That's okay. Let that disagreement be part of a positive discussion. Committed educators don't show up to work each day to make decisions they think will be bad for kids, so why would we want to use a phrase that conveys the message that we—the leaders—are the only ones who know best?

Another problem with the statement "I'm going to do what's best for kids," is that it has a finality to it that makes it hard for someone to respectfully disagree with you. It's a "last word" phrase, as opposed to a phrase that invites discussion and dialogue. After all, in our business, who wants to argue against doing what's best for kids?

Where does that argument stop? Using the earlier scenario of adding time to the school day to intervene for our third-grade readers, if thirty additional minutes per day is good, would an hour be better? Two? Maybe it would be best to have students come on Saturdays or during the winter break, or how about we just add four more weeks to the school year? Wouldn't that be "best"?

Another thing we wonder about is whether there really is one thing that's best for all kids? Isn't it more likely that what's best for one child may be different from what's best for another?

Who Are Your Primary Clients?

So what's the alternative? As school and district leaders, we all really want to do what's best for kids, so how do we go about that? If you are a school leader, you may serve hundreds or perhaps a thousand students in your school. If you are district leader, the number of students you serve may be well into the thousands. If you skip over or go around the adults in your system to try to do what's best for kids, you will never be able to maximize your impact on the students. So we offer this alternative: As a leader your ability to do "what's best for kids" often lies within your ability to inspire, influence, and support the adults in your school or system.

I (Shelley) was fortunate to spend ten years of my career working for Carol Parish, an exceptional "systems thinker." One of the many things I learned from Carol is that in our roles as leaders, we have to see beyond just our team, our school, our department. We have to understand how everything and everyone works together to make the whole system run if we want to be able to do our best work and inspire others to do theirs.

One of the most important things you can do as a leader in any role within the school system is to identify who your primary clients are and strategically plan ways to impact and support them to the best of your ability. When you ask educational leaders in almost any role who they believe to be their primary clients, the answer is often "the students." While, ultimately, the work you do needs to have a positive impact on students, we invite you to consider the following:

The primary clients for teachers should be students. Teachers are the ones who have daily contact with the students. As such, they have the opportunity to make the biggest impact on them. They are the ones who create the day-to-day learning environments and plan the daily learning experiences. The decisions they make on a regular basis will help determine whether students in their classrooms will flourish and thrive throughout the year. We know you want to make a positive impact on the students in your system, but the reality is you do not have the same capacity for influence on the students as teachers do.

The primary clients for school leaders should be teachers and staff. You can't teach every child in the school. You can't serve lunch to every child, tend to every scraped knee, answer every phone call, clean every classroom, or supervise every playground and hallway. But as a principal, you can have serious influence and a positive impact on how all of these things are done. If you are a school leader, make sure a significant amount of your time focuses on supporting the adults in your schools—helping them to be their best so they, in turn, can effectively serve their primary clients, the students.

The primary clients for central-office administrators should be principals and other site leaders. A leaders at the district level can't be the principal of every school. In district-office roles, your job often involves big-picture thinking so you can influence change across the entire system. To have system-wide impact, you need your principals on board. We have both observed systems that struggle because district office administrators leave principals either out of the loop or unsupported. No principal wants to be the "last to know." We have also seen systems struggle when new initiatives are introduced and principals aren't provided the necessary tools, information, learning, or support to lead the work at deep levels at their schools. If you are a district-level leader, your best opportunity to do what's best for kids is to support your site leadership so they can support the teachers who are working with your kids day in and day out.

WHAT'S "BEST" FOR KIDS CHALLENGE

- Who are your primary clients in your current role? How do you ensure that you are giving them the most support so that they can have the biggest impact on student learning?

- Who is your support system? Do you feel as though you get the needed support so that you can serve those you lead? If your answer is "no," how could you reach out and take steps to make this a reality? If the answer is "yes," how could you show appreciation for the support that is given?

 Share your thoughts, ideas, and artifacts with the *Lead Like a PIRATE* community using the #LeadLAP hashtag.

PROFESSIONAL DEVELOPMENT— LIKE A PIRATE!

Powerful professional development is the Archimedes lever that can move any school or district to the highest levels of success.
—Dave Burgess

Too many professional development initiatives are done to teachers, not for, with, or by them.
—Andy Hargreaves

It's time to rethink professional development time with our staff. In *Teach Like a PIRATE*, Dave asks the pivotal question for planning lessons: "If our students didn't have to be there, would we be teaching to an empty room?" Our question for you as a school leader is this: How can you ensure that if your staff didn't have to be there, the room would still be full?

Kicking up the Traditional Staff Meeting

Consider the questions below and use them as a launching point for transforming the typical staff professional learning into an experience that will carry over to make a true impact into instruction.

- How could you make it an experience that you could sell tickets to?

- How could you alter the room or setting to make the learning more meaningful?

- When planning the content, how could you make it relevant to everyone in attendance?

- How could voice and choice of participants be honored?

- How could you use a hook to pique interest or improve learning?

- If you were a participant in the training yourself, would you want to be there?

- How could you get prior input from the participants to help with your planning so you can personalize and differentiate the experience as much as possible?

- How could you ensure that the transformation would only add to the learning and not take away?

Speed Dating

At one of our professional-learning days this past school year, the leadership team and I (Beth) wanted to be sure that we devoted a portion of our time to the opportunity of learning new information. Collective professional development with staff is valuable for creating a common language and understanding, but offering staff members options for personalization of learning is also a priority in our building. One of our goals is to deepen our knowledge of best practice at the middle-school level. I first thought I would find an article to read and process together. As I browsed articles on amle.org, I realized that this was the perfect opportunity to let our staff choose the reading that best matched what they needed. The next question was how to transform the traditional read-and-respond method in our meeting. A few days earlier, I had seen a Tweet from a teacher in our building who showcased book "speed dating" as a means of helping students narrow down their next read. Her post sparked an idea about how I could do something similar with our staff. FMS Speed Dating PD was on its way to reality! Prior to the meeting, each staff member selected an article to read and took notes on the advanced organizer I provided.

We then revamped our meeting space (the library) to speed-dating central by moving our chairs into two circles to face each other. Everyone had three rounds to share their learning and then, in turn, gain learning from their colleagues. The first partner had ninety seconds to share the most important points from his/her article. The second partner then had thirty seconds to paraphrase (a norm of collaboration that we were practicing) and ask questions. Partners would then switch roles and repeat the process. I modeled this specifically before beginning and ran the timer on the SMART Board® to keep us on track.

After two rounds, I asked for feedback from staff on effectiveness of the structure. A few people shared ideas, and we adjusted and moved into the third and final round. During the feedback time, I pointed out that, although we often get formative assessment regarding the content we teach in our classrooms, it's rare that people ask for formative assessment on the methodology of delivering that content. Pausing between rounds allowed us all to immediately improve our delivery. We ended the session with reflections and continued sharing through our school hashtag.

Genius PD: Personalizing Professional Development

After reading Don Wettrick's book *Pure Genius: Building a Culture of Innovation and Taking 20 Percent Time to the Next Level*, several teachers at McIntire Elementary began to implement the idea of 20 percent time or Genius Hour in their classrooms. The format and structure of this time varied by classroom; some teachers dedicated time in each subject area for students to choose the means to learning the curricular standards, while other teachers gave students a specific time each week to explore whatever they were passionate about. We developed contracts and

PIRATE-Style PD

Speed Dating PD: bit.ly/FMSspeeddating
Personalized Learning Plan: bit.ly/PersPD
Reflection Form: bit.ly/PLReflectionLog
PD Twitter Chat: bit.ly/McTwitterChat

portfolios to track Genius Hour experiences so that it truly was seen as powerful, personalized student learning and not fluff. When these teachers and students were invited to showcase the Genius Hour examples at a school board meeting, the board members were in awe of the ownership of learning displayed by our students in their presentations.

As I (Beth) watched our students and teachers share their Genius Hour experiences, the wheels started turning in my mind: How could we transfer this successful practice of Genius Hour to adult learning in our school?

Beyond allowing for a choice in sessions during a PD day, I wanted to empower our staff to truly personalize their personal and professional development. I wanted to establish educator Genius Hour opportunities that allowed teachers to create, rather than simply consume, learning. Drawing on the power of my PLN (professional learning network), I reached out to some of the leading experts of Genius Hour implementation in schools. I talked to Joy Kirr (@JoyKirr) and Don Wettrick (@DonWettrick), asking them questions, studying their examples, paperwork, and ideas. With a solid idea of where to start, I rolled out the idea to our building leadership team for feedback. The team enthusiastically agreed that the idea of Genius PD time should be implemented immediately. Next, I shared the idea with our teachers who overwhelmingly supported the move to a differentiated professional development model that mirrored the Genius Hours happening in their classrooms.

Our staff then identified potential roadblocks. First and foremost, there would need to be a form of accountability to provide at the district and state level. Secondly, there would need to be a reflection piece to showcase the learning and implementation plans of the learning. I then worked to create a Personalized Learning Plan, with feedback from the leadership team for staff to complete prior to the Genius PD time. This plan was directly tied to the district and school goals and previous collective professional development that had been done together. I also created a reflection form to be filled out at the conclusion of the PD. An added twist of reflection was for the staff to complete a Twitter chat to showcase their reflection so everyone could see what was happening throughout the building.

Finally, it was time to make it happen! The personalized learning plan was sent out the week before the professional-development day. Each teacher completed the form, and I provided support and resources they identified in their plans. Round one of Genius PD was during the first half of a district PD day. The staff spent the first three hours of the day immersed in their own learning. I went around to offer support and then spent time on my own personalized learning as well, working to model the expectations set forth of staff. Afterward, everyone completed their reflection form and then met in the library, where I shared the Twitter chat instructions. Together, the staff took part in the first #McTeach Twitter chat. This first chat not only gave the staff a chance to reflect but also to see Twitter as a tool to connect with educators around the globe. This form of reflection was so powerful, in fact, that the staff actually led two chats (#tlap and #satchatwc) on shared leadership with hundreds of educators around the globe.

How could we transfer this successful practice of Genius Hour to adult learning in our school?

Before the next professional development day, I gathered feedback from the staff about how to make the second Genius PD even more successful. I worked with the leadership team to make these changes and eagerly anticipated Genius PD part two. When the day finally arrived, I was not able to get out of bed due to illness. I felt awful, but my absence provided an opportunity for the true power of Genius PD to shine.

Through the power of Twitter, I was able to lead the reflection chat from my bed. Staff joined the chat from their classrooms and small groups, further showcasing that powerful professional development—and building a collaborative, innovative, and empowering culture—can happen even when your staff isn't all in the same room.

Genius PD continued throughout the remainder of the year. Collective professional development was still an important piece of sustaining a powerful professional learning community; however, it was no longer the sole model of professional development for our staff.

Although I moved to the middle school the year following our implementation of personalized professional development, Genius PD is alive and well at McIntire Elementary. This model has also been brought to my new school to transform professional development there.

PROFESSIONAL DEVELOPMENT CHALLENGE

- Reflect: What is the current state of your typical staff meeting? Is it information getting? Could it be put in an email? If so, how could you shift to make this time for learning?

- Make a "no staff meetings that could simply be an email pledge" and dare to be different!

- Does your staff dread going to professional development? Do you? How could you transform current practices to get people running in, not out?

- How much time does your staff get for personalized PD? How could you make this happen on your campus?

 Share your thoughts, ideas, and artifacts with the *Lead Like a PIRATE* community using the #LeadLAP hashtag.

COACH LIKE A PIRATE

Coaching can be one of the most important, challenging, and rewarding aspects of leadership. In this section, we'll get into the nitty-gritty of staff evaluations, instructing, and redirection. Ultimately, we know that your goal—like ours—is to help every member of your crew be their very best. Sometimes that means you'll need to be a sounding board. Other times you may need to initiate coaching conversations. Read on to learn how to use ANCHOR Conversations to support positive, clear communication that invites feedback, collaboration, and improvement.

ANCHOR
CONVERSATIONS

Coaching is a form of professional development that brings out the best in people, uncovers strengths and skills, builds effective teams, cultivates compassion, and builds emotionally resilient educators. Coaching at its essence is the way that human beings, and individuals, have always learned best.
—Elena Aguilar, *The Art of Coaching*

We want to be able to look every parent in the eye and say to them, "At this school, it doesn't matter who your child's teacher is. Whoever it is, I guarantee that your child will have an amazing learning experience here." And we want to mean it!

One of the most essential roles of a school leader is supporting teachers in creating phenomenal classrooms. Doing that well requires spending time in classrooms as often as possible. And we can't just be okay at this part of our work; we have to be exceptional at it.

When you see your teachers in action, you will then have the opportunity to provide specific, high-quality feedback—feedback that can make a difference and influence practice. But too often, school and district leaders are unwelcome guests in classrooms. Teachers don't want us there. If they could, many of them would lock us out. Why is that? Maybe that's our fault. Think about it: How often and for what purpose do you typically visit classrooms? For most educational leaders, the answer is not very often and mostly for evaluation purposes. We visit because we have to, because we need to check off the boxes on the evaluation forms, and we must fulfill contractual obligations. Then, the bulk of any conversations we have around those observations are evaluative. From the teacher's point of view, a classroom visit by the principal means that the boss is there to check up, judge, and evaluate whether the teacher "meets or exceeds the standard of satisfactory performance." (No pressure!) If that is how we and our teachers view our time in classrooms, it's no wonder they don't want us there. And let's be honest: it's part of why we don't want to go. So instead we find other (less) important business to take up our time.

When observations and feedback are designed to be evaluative and judgmental, they leave people with a sick feeling in the pit of their stomachs. Teachers see us as people who come into their classrooms with a fix-it mentality—and no one really wants to be fixed.

Do you? We don't.

Even if we don't mean to, when we step into our leadership roles and feel the weight of being responsible for *everything*, we too easily slip into fix-it mode. Maybe you can relate: Suddenly, everything that's wrong stands out, and we feel an overwhelming urge to tell people (not ask or guide or encourage, but tell) people how to make it right. We become the chief fixers, the final judges, the buck-stops-here evaluators. What a daunting task! It's no wonder that most school leaders hate the evaluation process almost as much as our teachers do!

Like it or not, evaluations are a necessary part of school leadership. We get that. But we also know that evaluations **cannot** be the driving force behind (and only reason for) classroom visits and conversations about teaching and learning. If every visit you make and every conversation you have is for the purpose of evaluation, you can bet that you aren't being invited into the real conversations about teaching and learning in your school or district. People who work for you have probably learned how to "talk the talk" to impress you. They will "walk the talk" on the days you visit so they can earn their check marks and get on with what they perceive to be the real business of teaching and learning after you walk out that door.

As a PIRATE leader, your goal is to avoid causing these fake, unfruitful conversations and staged visits like the plague. Because the treasure is to be invited into the *real* conversations about teaching and learning. To help your teachers and students succeed, you need to know about the real challenges people face and the obstacles that are getting in their way. You want them to share the fears and work struggles that keep them up at night. Only then will you be able to effectively support them.

When leaders focus primarily on evaluation, the staff feels that leaders are judging them and everything they do, and the teachers worry: *Am I wrong? Am I good enough?* Rather than being judged as lacking, they hide their challenges and struggles. Sadly, their leaders will never be given the opportunity to work alongside them and help them learn and grow. If evaluation is your main focus, people will not be vulnerable with you; and without some level of vulnerability, you won't be able to help them get better at their craft.

Changing culture requires changing the conversations.

Nobody wants to be fixed, but we do believe that just about everyone loves to learn and grow! People like to get better at what they do; they want to be better tomorrow than they were today. In fact, we believe that most people are hungry for the kind of feedback that pushes them and challenges them to think in different ways about their practice. If you want to dramatically transform your school or district culture to one where everyone is committed to taking risks and trying new things—and where people ask for and accept feedback that will help them learn and grow—you have to remove the anxiety associated with observations and feedback. Changing culture requires changing the conversations.

ANCHOR Conversations: A Mindset Shift

So, if not evaluative feedback, what can you do instead? Use what we call ANCHOR Conversations! We have both been students of coaching throughout our time as educational leaders. We have read countless books and attended many professional-development sessions on coaching and giving feedback. We have learned from some of the best, people like Madeline Hunter, Carolyn Downey, Richard Elmore, Elena Aguilar, Jerry Valentine, Vickie Robb, Bob Hogan, Huck Fitterer, and Sue Harwood, among others. We are relentless about increasing our knowledge and expertise in this area because we have seen firsthand the dramatic impact that high-quality coaching can have on people—especially in an environment that values learning, practice, growth, and reflection. Great coaching is a game changer.

During the past several years, we have drawn on what we have learned, as well as our personal experiences as educational leaders, to design a coaching model based on what has been proven to work for us and our schools and district. Collectively, we have observed thousands of lessons and we have used those observations as springboards for *meaningful conversations* about teaching and learning with teachers, coaches, principals, and many others.

> *ANCHOR conversations begin well*
> *before you even set foot in*
> *your teachers' classrooms—*
> *and they start with you.*

An ANCHOR conversation, at its core, is a mindset shift for observing classrooms and then engaging in dialogue about what you saw. However, ANCHOR conversations begin well before you even set foot in your teachers' classrooms—and they start with you. They begin with an honest and in-depth reflection of your own belief system about the people who work for you: Do you *really* believe in them? All of them—not just your superstars? Do you believe they have what it takes to be *amazing* educators? Do you believe they want to thrive? That they *can* thrive?

Disclaimer: For ANCHOR conversations to work, you have to start with a mindset that each member of your staff is *capable* of making magic happen in their classrooms. ANCHOR conversations may not be for you if:

- You are a principal who, when looking at your staff, thinks, *Our school or our system would be awesome if only we had some different teachers.*

- You are a leader in a district-office position who, when looking at your principals and other leaders, thinks, *Our district would be so amazing and impactful if only we had some different principals.*

- You focus on *what's wrong with them* and how their faults are getting in your way.

ANCHOR conversations represent a shift away from the judgmental, fix-it mentality and toward a mentality that notices people's strengths and commits to building off those strengths with the desire to move each individual forward.

The ANCHOR conversation framework is what we use with most people, most of the time. However, it is *not* the framework we use when there are serious red flags or if we notice something egregious, harmful, or that in any way needs our immediate attention. We will be the first to acknowledge that sometimes it's necessary to take off the coach hat, put on the evaluator/supervisor hat, and have difficult, courageous conversations. While it is never fun, we have both had to write up people, tell people their work isn't up to par, and even coach people out of the profession. It's never easy, but we both know it is a critical part of our role as leaders.

Fortunately, in our experience, those evaluative SOS conversations are the exception rather than the rule. Most of the time, people are doing good work, or at least trying really hard to do so. ANCHOR conversations help those people move from good, to better, to great!

Three Goals of ANCHOR Conversations

At the heart of the ANCHOR conversation framework are the goals we have as we enter into conversations with folks. It is critical to understand these goals and to keep them front and center because they will help you build the kind of positive culture we advocate for in schools and school systems. We are assuming that you want to create a culture where staff, not just students, are running to get in the doors. Understanding the needs of the adults in your system is essential to creating this kind of school culture and pushing practice forward. With that in mind, we have three primary goals for every ANCHOR conversation.

Goal One

Every time we engage in a conversation with a crew member, we want them to walk away knowing **we value them** for the work they do day in and day out to change our students' lives.

Goal Two

After the conversation, we want them to walk away believing that **we added value**. We want each person on our team to see us as a resource, as someone who knows a lot about teaching and learning and who has good ideas to share. We want the teacher to know that we can be a good sounding board and that we will listen without passing judgment. We want them to know we are capable of asking good questions that might push their thinking or cause them to reflect on something a little bit differently. We want them to walk away from a conversation with us feeling like it was worth it—and actually looking forward to the next time they get to have a conversation with us. Better yet, we want them to *seek us out* when they are working on a new or innovative idea for their classroom because they think a conversation with us might strengthen it and make it even better.

Goal Three

We want our conversations with teachers to **push practice forward**. If a person leaves the conversation excited about what we talked about and anxious to try out one of those ideas or practices tomorrow or next week—mission accomplished! We love it when coaching conversations lead to implementation. Inspiration is great, but as Dave says, "Inspiration without implementation is a waste." To make an impact and create change, our conversations have to be more than just about building positive relationships; they have to influence and push practice forward.

ANCHOR Conversations

ANCHOR conversations have six components. Each component can work together in one conversation on one day and stand alone on another, but all aspects are important if we want to enthusiastically coach people forward in their work.

A is for Appreciation.

Appreciation can make a day, even change a life. Your willingness to put it into words is all that is necessary.
—Margaret Cousins

We need to give daily messages of appreciation. People do not get enough of it in our profession. Schools and educators are a popular target for negativity, and let's be honest, even within our own schools and systems, negativity can be an issue.

Not too long ago, I (Shelley) had the opportunity to do a full-day workshop for a group of new and aspiring principals with a colleague of mine. One component of the workshop focused on the critical responsibility of principals to visit classrooms often and to engage teachers in meaningful conversations about teaching and learning that motivate and inspire. As part of this seminar, we shared ideas about what to look for during classroom visits and ways to shape meaningful conversations around the teaching and learning happening in the classroom. We also watched video clips of classroom teachers and their students during lessons and asked the participants to discuss what they observed from each lesson. We then role-played conversations where one person took on the role of the teacher and another took on the role of administrator.

As participants started this role-playing activity, my colleague and I were disheartened with many of the comments we heard. They were negative, judgmental, and examples of that fix-it mentality. They went straight to what they thought was wrong with a lesson while ignoring all the things that were going right. Their lack of appreciation for any of the good they saw happening in a lesson led to uninspiring feedback where they were simply telling the teacher what they thought she should do. The lessons we watched were not perfect, but what lesson ever is? It definitely had components that might be worthy of discussion on how to strengthen and enhance the experience for the students, but there was also a lot to appreciate.

One lesson we watched was given by a middle-school social studies teacher who was trying the strategy of close reading with a text. Granted, she was struggling a bit, but it was also admittedly something new she was trying to do with her students. While most of the new and aspiring administrators in the room were intently focused on what they didn't like about the lesson, here are the first few things my colleague and I appreciated about what we saw:

- The teacher allowed a camera into her room to film her lesson.
- She was taking a risk and trying a new strategy.
- She was trying to give more ownership of the learning to the students.
- She was structuring time for students to talk to one another about a complex text to try to make meaning of it.
- She tried to have kids use context clues to figure out word meanings.
- She was checking in with the groups; she noticed when they were struggling and brought them back together as a whole group to model her thinking as she read a section to them.

- She identified the major error the kids were making and adjusted her instruction to try to help them through their struggle.
- And we appreciated a lot more!

Was this the most polished close reading lesson I've ever seen? No. Could her lesson have used refinement? Absolutely. My guess is she knew her lesson and approach needed work. As educators, we are often our own worst critics!

The teaching of new standards, trying new strategies, doing something different require practice, reflection, feedback, refinement, more practice, more feedback, more reflection, and so on! If we don't notice and appreciate the risk taking, the practices, the approximation, the trying on of new things, and instead we immediately judge best efforts and first attempts as poor or unsatisfactory, many teachers will stop trying and fall back on the things they already know. Then we'll be left to sit back and wonder why nothing is changing in our classrooms and schools.

Be intentional about developing an appreciation for what you see.

If you are fortunate enough to be in a role that allows you to visit classrooms often and engage with teachers in conversations about the teaching and learning happening in their classrooms, be intentional about developing an appreciation for what you see. With the thousands of lessons I (Shelley) have observed, I can quickly think of just two observations where I genuinely couldn't find anything to appreciate. Both were while I was in the role of assistant superintendent and walking through classrooms with principals. The first was an observation of a primary-grade classroom. When the principal and I walked into the classroom, the teacher was nowhere to be found. I don't know how long she was gone before we got there, but she returned eight minutes and thirty-seven seconds after we arrived, with a steaming hot cup of coffee in her hand, looked at us, and thanked us for watching her class. She had literally just left her classroom full of young kids alone for at least eight minutes and thirty-seven seconds to get coffee.

The second observation where I struggled to find something to appreciate was also in a primary classroom. I walked into the classroom at 2:02 and the school day ended at 2:30. Students were milling around, sitting and chatting, basically doing whatever they wanted with no direction. When I asked the teacher to share with me a little bit about what was going on, she told me that I might want to come back tomorrow because she "stops teaching at 2:00." *What!?*

Other than those two vivid examples (that still can keep me up at night), I have always been able to find something to appreciate. No, not every lesson we've observed has been award-winning, but just about every one of them has had merit and has had something about it that we could appreciate. We just have to look for it. When we do, we are always amazed by how many positive things we can find.

So that's where ANCHOR conversations start. They start with giving messages of appreciation. And these messages of appreciation go beyond a "Great job!" or a "You're awesome!" They have specific components to them that make them powerful coaching messages as well as just great messages for people to hear. Below is a sample message of appreciation:

> *I was so excited to be in your classroom today. Thank you so much for letting me learn with you and your students. I just wanted to tell you how much I appreciated the thoughtful, juicy questions you posed to your students today. They really got your students to think deeply while also building their excitement and curiosity about the topic. Thank you for taking the extra time to think so deeply about engaging, higher-level questions to ask your students.*

Notice how that goes beyond a simple "thank you" or an "I loved when you did_____." It actually has some powerful coaching components embedded in it.

Critical Components of a Powerful "ANCHOR of Appreciation"

1. **Share something the teacher did that you appreciated. Pick something specific and label it!**

   Calling out a specific practice by name and showing appreciation for it brings it to the forefront of the teacher's thinking. That simple awareness makes it more likely that the teacher will think about the practice when planning their next lesson. Labeling the practice gives the teacher the language to use the next time they are planning a lesson collaboratively with a colleague. They are now more likely to remember the practice and share it with others: "Hey, I think we should come up with some thoughtful, juicy questions that will get kids excited about the topic."

2. **Tell them specifically why you appreciated it.**

3. **Link the "why" to best practices, school goal, and/or student learning.**

   Adding a statement of why and linking it to best practice or school goals or student learning elevates your message. At the time that the message above was delivered, one of the school's stated goals was to increase student engagement and ask questions that required higher levels of thinking. Through this message of appreciation, that school goal was restated and reinforced. By making the connection, the teacher is also affirmed by the message that "I'm noticing that what you are trying and doing supports the collective goals we have, and I am saying thank you for making that commitment."

4. **Smile and use an enthusiastic tone, upbeat word choices, and positive body language.**

   Word choice, body language, tone of voice all matter! Use all of them to convey enthusiasm about what you saw. That enthusiastic, upbeat energy is contagious. The more excited you are to talk about teaching and learning, the more excited they will be to talk about it as well.

5. **Say "Thank you!" Thanking people for the work they do is important, and we simply can't do it often enough!**

We affectionately call this "dropping ANCHORs of Appreciation" with our staff. We can tell you that dropping these ANCHORs can be the one of the best parts of our day. It's also a way for us to recalculate when we get off course. Sometimes we get so busy as administrators that we truly forget to sit back, relax, and watch the amazing things that are happening in front of us in classrooms each day. Be intentional and take thirty minutes a day to just drop these anchors of appreciation throughout the school.

Messages of appreciation can easily be given face-to-face right before you leave the classroom or in passing as you walk by a teacher in the hall. You can also leave a quick note on the teacher's desk or in his or her inbox. Here's a simple template that can easily be copied and modified: bit.ly/leadappreciation. *Tip*: Leave these messages with students to give to your staff members. This builds a culture of appreciation. Our students see far too many examples of negativity. We have to be the models of the positive change that is needed in our schools, and the world beyond, and we can do that by involving them (even in small ways) in showing appreciation.

Do not feel like you have to limit your appreciation messages to just what is happening in the classroom. It's easy to find things to appreciate with staff outside classrooms as they participate in IEP meetings, bus duty, lunch duty, and work together on behavior interventions and in team meetings. It is amazing how much there is to appreciate when you take time to look for it.

A Few Cannonballs to Avoid

- Avoid judgment language. Liking something is not the same as appreciating it

- Avoid false praise. Once you share your appreciation for something, it will be repeated so choose wisely.

- Avoid dropping ANCHORS of appreciation to the same people over and over while forgetting others. We can find something to appreciate about every one of our crew.

APPRECIATION CHALLENGE

Take just thirty minutes out of your day and visit fifteen classrooms for two minutes each. Before you leave each classroom, tell the teacher something you appreciated about what you just saw. Nothing you say should be about what you think should be better; this time is strictly for messages of appreciation. In the words of Anthony Robbins, "Where your focus goes, your energy flows." As leaders we have been conditioned to look for what needs to be better. We are "fixers" by nature, but if that is where we focus all of our attention, we are at risk of missing all that is going right. The best-kept secret about dropping fifteen ANCHORs of appreciation is that you will not only brighten your teachers' day, but you'll feel pretty good yourself!

 Share your thoughts, ideas, and artifacts with the *Lead Like a PIRATE* community using the #LeadLAP hashtag.

N is for Notice the Impact.

One must always be aware, to notice—even though the cost of noticing is to become responsible.
—Thylias Moss

Have you ever asked a phenomenal teacher how he or she does what they do? It often seems so natural to them. Their work is such a part of who they are that they often can't really describe it to you. It's like trying to describe to someone how to tie your shoe; it has become such a habit that it can be difficult to tell people how we do it. Believe it or not, it was actually this concept that ultimately led Dave to write and publish *Teach Like a PIRATE*. One of his good friends was planning a series of workshops for teachers in their district and wanted Dave to present. His friend knew Dave was a phenomenal teacher, but he wasn't sure Dave could teach others to do what he did. Dave took this as a challenge and became relentless about figuring out how to do so. He was constantly thinking about his thinking as he planned his lessons during the next year. Not long afterward, *Teach Like a PIRATE* was born.

This piece of the ANCHOR conversation model is so critical in ensuring that the feedback you give helps build self-efficacy and encourages teachers to continue powerful practices in a very deliberate and intentional way. The mindset shift in this one is that observation/evaluation time is not about noticing things you like or dislike in a lesson and sharing those with the teacher; it's about noticing and pointing out the decisions they make that have a positive impact on learning.

Observation time is about noticing and pointing out the decisions teachers make that have a positive impact on learning.

Instead of judgment language, try using "noticing" language. This is language that acknowledges that the teacher made a choice to do something, and that choice had a significant and specific impact on the learning experience for students. Comment on decisions the teacher made and their impact. Doing so builds that sense of self-efficacy. Your teachers will realize that *every choice matters*, and that they hold the power in their hands to unlock amazing potential in each one of the students in their classes.

We are convinced that people actually feel a greater sense of satisfaction when we drop a "Notice the Impact" ANCHOR than if we were just to say "great job" or "awesome lesson"—especially when we notice impact and connect it to sound pedagogy and effective practice.

So what does it sound like to drop this ANCHOR? Something like this ...

> *I'm so excited to be able to catch up with you for a minute! I wanted to tell you that when I was in your classroom today, I noticed you made a choice to add visuals and pictures to your lesson on habitats. I sat down next to Maria (an English learner in the class). When you first started talking about the desert habitat, she was having a hard time following, but as soon as you started to show the pictures, she totally got it and was quickly able to add words and pictures to her notes. I literally saw the light bulb go on over her head! Thank you for doing that. Every time you present your content in more than one way, you increase the chances that every child will learn what you are trying to teach them. I'd love to hear more about some of your upcoming lessons and how you are using a variety of modalities to get your message across!*

and

> *I was so fortunate to be in your classroom for a few minutes today when your students were reading and discussing the article on the Statue of Liberty. You had just made the decision to pose the questions: "Why do you think the Statue of Liberty serves as*

a symbol of hope? Are there other symbols of hope in our society? Justify your thinking." I sat down with group one, and they were having a powerful and thoughtful discussion. Because you posed questions that did not have a right or wrong answer, you encouraged more complex thinking and allowed for divergent thinking, and in the group I sat with, every child had something wonderful to contribute. I'd love to come by and see another collaborative student discussion about their reading. Do you have another one planned soon?

One of the primary goals of noticing impact is to bring awareness to the decisions teachers make. If they've been teaching for a while, they may not realize or be able to articulate some of the choices they have made ... they just come naturally to them or are just a "part of what they do." Making them cognizant of their choices and then pointing out how those decisions made a positive impact helps ensure that these good practices happen as the result of deliberate planning rather than by chance. Similar to the messages of appreciation, noticing impact messages also helps to label practices and connect the work a teacher is doing to effective practice and school goals.

Critical Components of a Powerful Noticing Impact Message

1. **Share something specific that you noticed the teacher do and label it as their decision or their choice.**

Specificity is important. It prevents your message from getting lost in generalities. Be specific about the decision and the fact that they made a deliberate choice. Nothing is left to chance in a classroom. It may feel like that to teachers sometimes, but they are ultimately in control of just about everything that happens in their room. Bring awareness to the reality that they are always making decisions and choices. This reminder helps them understand that basically everything that happens in the classroom is the result of a choice made by the teacher—and that awareness helps put the power back in the teacher's hands. Sometimes a classroom can feel out of control. If teachers feel as if they have no power over the situation, it's unlikely that they will take steps to improve what seems to them like a lost cause. What's the point of wasting all that effort? But if you can remind them that every choice—every action or inaction—matters, you can build a culture where people feel empowered to take steps every day to learn and grow. And that's when your teachers will start to believe that they *do* have the power to create something amazing.

2. **Share the impact of the choice.**

Pointing out the impact of your teachers' choices draws a straight line between the decision and the outcome. We know too many humble teachers who don't own the positive impact they make on kids. Phenomenal student learning, highly engaged students, well-behaved students—none of these happen by accident. They aren't a result of just having "good kids this year." Positive outcomes occur because teachers make choices that have impact. Connect the dots for them between their choice and the impact it has. Do this over and over and over again. Make it abundantly clear that what teachers choose to do matters.

3. **Link the impact to student learning, sound pedagogy, and/or school goals.**

Just like with appreciation, adding a statement of *why* and linking it to best practices, school goals, or student learning elevates your message of noticing the impact. Every opportunity you get to link what you observed to the choices teachers make, you are helping each individual grow and learn while at the same time helping move the whole school forward.

Let's look at the first sample message above. When I (Shelley) did this observation, I knew that the decision to add the visual components to the lesson was an afterthought. I could just tell by how it was done that it was not preplanned. He really wasn't thinking about impacting English learners when he did it, and I know that. But by choosing to call that out as what I noticed—the impact it had on the student I was sitting next to—and then linking it to the sound pedagogical practice of presenting information in more than one way, I was actually coaching and teaching in a very positive way. And what I know from subsequent observations is that the teacher became more deliberate about adding visuals and other modalities of learning into his lessons. And I noticed them and shared their impact with him every time I saw them, which in turn reinforced him to do it even more often.

4. **Encourage continued use of the practice.**

You can encourage continued use of a positive practice by simply saying that you are looking forward to seeing more of that practice in the future because it makes a positive impact on learning. The ongoing use of seemingly small but impactful practices can ultimately make a dramatic transformation in a classroom.

5. **Smile and use an enthusiastic tone, upbeat word choice, and positive body language.**

Word choice, body language, tone of voice still matter. Convey enthusiasm about the impactful choices the teacher is making.

6. **Say "Thank you!"—again.**

It's just that important to thank people!

Another way to use the notice the impact component of ANCHOR conversations is to reinforce risk taking among your staff members. When you observe a teacher trying out something new, tell them you noticed and that you appreciate the impact it had. Oftentimes, when a practice is new, teachers get caught up in trying to do it right. If it doesn't go as they had hoped, they may give up and go back to their old ways. So every time you notice a teacher step out of their comfort zone to try to improve, learn, and grow, notice it, appreciate it, and support it if it has potential to make a positive impact on student learning.

It is extremely popular, almost cliché, for leaders to say they support risk taking and innovation. But your crew members don't know if you *really* support risk taking until they see how you respond when someone fails. It's easy to support risk taking when people are successful, but when people are truly taking risks, eventually someone will fail and fall face first. How you respond will determine whether you see more or less risk taking and innovation in your system.

A Few Cannonballs to Avoid

- Avoid judgment language. It's not about what you like, it's about impactful practice.
- Avoid false praise. You don't want to encourage continuation of bad practice.
- Avoid lack of clarity or generalities on the sound pedagogy or practice. If you can't describe it, choose something else. Saying "It helped students learn" is not specific enough.

Notice the Impact Challenge

Take thirty minutes to visit six to eight classrooms for three or four minutes each. Identify a choice or decision the teacher has made and "Notice the Impact." Drop that ANCHOR and let them know the decisions they make have impact! (While you're at it, add an A is for Appreciation message into your feedback as well!)

 Share your thoughts, ideas, and artifacts with the *Lead Like a PIRATE* community using the #LeadLAP hashtag.

C is for Collaborative Conversations.

If you want to go fast, go alone.
If you want to go far, go together.
—African Proverb

It isn't uncommon to feel as if the weight of your schools rests squarely and solely on your shoulders. But the reality is that you are surrounded by teams of people in your schools and districts who have incredible expertise in a wide variety of areas. As a PIRATE leader, we encourage (implore!) you to free yourself from thinking you have to know, do, and be everything. Instead, we want you to tap into the multitude of talents, gifts, and expertise that lie within each and every person who works with you. Unleashing the genius of those around you ultimately contributes to a thriving culture where people feel valued and are willing to learn and grow individually and as part of a crew. And as you open yourself to learning from and with your crew members, you will continue to develop greater expertise.

Collaborative conversations are coaching conversations, not evaluative ones.

This idea that we aren't the only experts in the building is the foundation for the Collaborative Conversations component of ANCHOR. As mentioned earlier, while there are times when direct feedback is essential, we have found that engaging in collaborative conversations about teaching and learning has a powerful impact on a person's willingness to try something new, to learn, and to grow. Collaborative conversations are much more likely to help you build a culture of commitment as opposed to a culture of compliance.

Collaborative conversations are coaching conversations, not evaluative ones. During these two-way conversations, you and the teacher work as partners to figure out what was successful about a lesson and what elements might need tweaking. The conversation is about brainstorming together and sharing ideas. During these conversations, you and the teacher are on equal ground; your opinions and ideas don't necessarily have any more merit than the ideas the teacher puts forth. Sometimes the teacher has the better idea, and other times you do. By asking good questions and listening to understand, you can work with your teacher to find the best solution or practice. Most of all, collaborative conversations should be fun. They are an opportunity to roll up your sleeves and just talk about good teaching and learning in a way that inspires you both. Here's an example of how a collaborative conversation might begin:

> *It was so fun to be in your classroom yesterday and see that all of the students were working on their Chromebooks. I really appreciate that you are working hard to integrate the new technology into your classroom! I didn't get the opportunity to stay very long, but it looked like you had set up an opportunity for the students to work collaboratively in groups using Google Docs. I'd love to hear more about what they were doing ...*

Additional questions asked during this conversation could include:

> *How have you liked working with the Chromebooks? How's it going for you?*

> *What's the biggest difference you have noticed since you started using the technology?*

> *How have the students responded to using the Chromebooks?*

> *So you have had students collaborating using Google Docs pretty regularly. What are some of the other ways you have been thinking about incorporating the technology into your lessons?*

At this point in the conversation there is an exchange of ideas. The teacher shares some thoughts and you share others. Once you have talked through a few good ideas, the next step in the conversation should be a call to action:

> *Wow! So many powerful ideas have come out of this conversation. Which one do you think you'll try next?*

After the teacher shares the approach or idea he/she wants to implement, your response should both be encouraging and provide an opportunity for accountability.

> *That sounds like it would be a natural next step, and I think your students would really benefit from it. Would you mind shooting me an email when you are going to try it out? I'd love to come by and see how the kids respond!*

Critical Components of a Collaborative Conversation

1. Give a message of appreciation.

We recommend dropping an ANCHOR of appreciation first as it's always a great way to kick off any conversation.

2. Ask a question or invite conversation based on what you observed.

One of the most important things you can do as an educational leader is hone your questioning skills. The person who does the most talking and reflecting is the one who is doing the most learning. In any collaborative conversation, the majority of the talking should be done by the teacher, so that means you need to be exceptional at asking questions that push thinking and require deeper levels of reflection.

3. **Respond to what the teacher shares, share your thoughts, and ask another question.**

When the teacher responds to a question, listen intently and then respond. Ask clarifying questions if you have them. If the teacher shares something you know is highly effective practice, label it for them, and share the reasons why you know it works for kids. If they share an idea that sparks one in you, share that too, and then continue to ask questions that let the conversation build. You can go back and forth this way as long as it continues to move the learning and reflection forward. It is so much more powerful for us to engage in two-way conversations that lead to an abundance of good ideas than it is for us to observe and then tell them one idea we think they should implement.

Oftentimes in these conversations, the teacher will share a struggle they are having or they share an idea that makes them a little nervous or that they aren't 100 percent sure how to implement. First, tell them how much you appreciate their sharing the struggle and acknowledge that it is a great thing to be thinking about. Then, brainstorm solutions together and ask how you could help.

4. **Encourage the teacher to try one of the new ideas that came out of your conversation.**

The goal for collaborative conversations is to push practice. That's why we always try and add a "soft layer of accountability" by asking the teacher something like: "So what do you think you will do next?" or, "When do you think you will try that?" or by saying, "I would love for you to let me know how it goes!" Better yet, ask when they are going to try it out and offer to pop in to see how it goes.

Teachers are busy people. Trying out new things takes time, planning, and preparation. It is easy for any of us to walk away from an energizing conversation, a great exchange of ideas on Twitter, or a good education conference filled with new ideas that we want to try but ultimately never do. A promise to someone else that we will give it a shot is sometimes all it takes to move something from being just a good idea to being something good we actually do.

5. Say "Thank you!"

If done well, these collaborative conversations can be energizing for you and the person with whom you are collaborating, so thank them for their time and for pushing your learning as well.

 A Few Cannonballs to Avoid

- Don't make assumptions about what came before the time you observed or what happened after. Ask a question instead: "When I walked in, kids were doing _____. Tell me a little about what happened before I came in the room. How did it go after I left?"

- Don't do most of the talking. Remember this is a *collaborative* conversation. Shoot for a minimum of a 50/50 balance of talking and listening.

- Don't try to mask criticism as a question; people will see right through you.

COLLABORATIVE CONVERSATION CHALLENGE

Choose one or two days this week where you set aside thirty minutes to visit classrooms and thirty minutes to engage in collaborative conversations with the teachers whose classrooms you visited. Visit each classroom for five to ten minutes and then let the teacher know: "Thank you so much for having me in your classroom today; I always learn so much when I visit! I'd love to chat with you about the lesson I observed today. Do you have some time later when we can do that?"

Have fun with this challenge! The one-on-one time we get with our teachers is rare and oh so precious! Appreciate and enjoy the time you have together.

C Is Also for . . .
Captain-Directed Conversations.

While we love having collaborative conversations with people, sometimes the situation calls for a more captain-directed conversation. Captain-directed conversations are the ones you have when you realize the teacher really needs your help. They are struggling with something and just can't get it right, or they are trying something and are missing a few steps that maybe they don't understand and need clarification from you. A good way to look at a captain-directed conversation is as an instructional conversation where you are teaching something to the other person.

A quick example is a conversation I (Shelley) had with a teacher where he couldn't understand why so many students struggled with the work he had assigned after he had just taught a lesson. In our conversation, he shared with me that he had checked for understanding (this is something we had been working on) and that through this process he thought they all understood the lesson, so he couldn't figure out why they struggled so much when they moved to more independent practice.

Because I had observed the lesson, I knew he had actually missed a few steps in the "checking for understanding" process. He had the students do a group task to check for understanding. Since what he really wanted to know was whether each individual student understood the material, the answers generated by groups didn't give him what he was looking for. In any given group, as long as one student understood the material, the task could get done, and it *appeared* that everyone understood when, in fact, they didn't.

Once he told me he thought he had done a "check for understanding," it allowed me to move into instructional mode and teach him the elements that have to be in place to check for the kind of understanding he was looking for. We didn't need to brainstorm; I just needed to teach him the components of checking for understanding and then point out why the group work didn't meet that set of criteria. Once I taught him the elements, I asked him to share with me what he could do tomorrow to get a better understanding of what each individual student knows and doesn't know about the content. As he explained what he might do, I helped him refine the process until it consisted of the elements he needed. I also let him know I'd stop back by his class the next day to observe him trying it out just in case he needed any additional help.

Components of Captain-Directed Conversations

1. **Label and define the practice that was missing or that the teacher was struggling to execute.**

One of the things that can trip us up in coaching conversations, or in any conversations about teaching and learning for that matter, is the use of education buzzwords and jargon. Educators throw around phrases and terms all the time, terms like *student engagement, checking for understanding, formative assessment, rigorous instruction,* etc. We think everyone knows what they mean, but the reality is these can all mean very different things to different educators. The better we are at labeling practices when we see them and then *defining them,* the more likely we are to all come to a common understanding of what the words and phrases mean in our school communities. Having a common language and understanding of practices can help us avoid misunderstandings and conflicts with our staff.

> *A common language and understanding of practices can help prevent misunderstandings and conflicts.*

In the example above, the teacher had labeled the practice as a "check for understanding," but his understanding or definition for that phrase was not accurate. That misunderstanding led him to get results with his students that he wasn't expecting. Part of the captain-directed conversation included a definition of "checking for understanding," as well as instruction on the criteria that needed to be in place for a true "check." In the end, he walked away with a better understanding of what the term meant and how to use this practice more effectively in his classroom.

2. Share examples of what the practice could/should look like.

This is simply good teaching. When you are providing instruction or teaching something new to someone, give lots of examples in multiple contexts. It's important to give a couple of examples of what it could have looked like in the context of the lesson you just observed.

3. Explain the impact on student learning.

This is also a critical step. As part of the conversation, you are asking the teacher to do something differently—to adjust the way he teaches in some way. Offering the justification for that in terms of student-learning impact is important. If people are making changes, they want to see results. In the example above, the teacher had tried it his way and didn't get the results he had hoped for and expected. He wanted more accurate information about how his students were grasping the content he was teaching, so there was a good reason for him to want to learn something new, and he was willing to give it a shot.

4. Check for understanding.

Again, this is just good teaching. After providing instruction or clarification on a practice, it's always a good idea to find out whether the person you are working with understands what you were sharing in the way that you intended them to. It could be something as simple as asking, "So when you plan your lesson for tomorrow, what do you think you'll do to check for student understanding?" and "How is that different from what you did today?" If they have a good understanding of the practice, tell them so! If they don't, continue to teach and clarify.

5. Schedule a follow-up visit to see the new practice in action.

You entered into a captain-directed conversation because the teacher was struggling with something. Even after the conversation, don't assume that they've got it down. We all need practice when we are doing something new, so make yourself available to be back in the classroom soon to observe the practice and offer more support.

6. Say "Thank you!"

In this instance, the thank-you we give is often a thank-you for wanting to learn and grow and to continuously get better at this complex task we call teaching. And it's a thank you for trusting us enough to share a struggle.

 ## A Few Cannonballs to Avoid

- Don't have a captain-directed conversation based on observing something you "didn't like." They are for something you observed where the teacher needs help or clarification.

- Avoid making these conversations "evaluative" in nature. It is okay for someone not to "get" everything - be a support, not a hammer.

- Don't use a captain-directed coaching conversation when you *should* be having a courageous S.O.S. conversation. When something is seriously wrong, treat it as such.

CAPTAIN-DIRECTED CONVERSATION CHALLENGE

What are instances that constitute a conversation that must be captain-directed? What is it about these instances that makes them a barrier to student learning?

Think back to a conversation you have had with a staff member that had to be captain-directed. What went well? What did not go so great? Look back at this section and identify one practice you will begin doing the next time you have to have a conversation that is directed by you.

 Share your thoughts, ideas, and artifacts with the *Lead Like a PIRATE* community using the #LeadLAP hashtag.

H is for Honor Voice and Choice.

One of the most sincere forms of respect is actually listening to what another has to say.
—Bryant H. McGill

When you have an effective collaborative conversation or even a captain-directed one, many good ideas have come out of it. Honoring voice and choice means that you now turn the decision making over to the teacher. We always recommend closing out these conversations with a question like, "Which of these ideas do you find most intriguing?" or "So, where do you think you'd like to go next?" Once you've asked the question, let the teacher tell you! Too often classroom observations result in those "telling" conversations. We share what we saw, what we liked and what we didn't like, and we make a recommendation for something the teacher should do next or do differently.

Why do we do that? As PIRATE leaders, we want amazing instruction and incredible learning experiences happening in every classroom every day, and there are so many pathways to making that happen—not just the one that we see. Yes, you need to hold tightly to your expectations of sound and effective pedagogy, lessons, and experiences that stretch and engage your students. And you must keep a focus on the specific school goals for teaching and learning. But you don't need to hand people a script or a rulebook to follow in order to reach those goals.

We want people who work for us to be excited to come to work each day. We want them to be excited about trying something new and passionate about their own learning and growth. We want them to stretch themselves and do things that they once didn't even think they were capable of doing. Part of making that happen is giving them voice and choice. Allow them to decide how to bring those incredible learning experiences into their classrooms.

We are so over the lockstep, scripted, be-on-the-same-page-on-the-same-day type of teaching that has been going on in schools across the country for years, and frankly, so are most teachers. Be deeply committed to creating schools and classrooms where great learning is happening for students on a daily basis in every classroom, but be careful what you hold people accountable for. Rather than holding people accountable for being on page fifty-five this Thursday, choose to hold people accountable for learning, for making the commitment to continuously grow and get better, and to making an even greater impact on their students tomorrow than they did today. Be crystal clear about what your goals are, and make sure that everyone on your team knows what they are as well. Then give as much leeway as possible to your teams and individual teachers so they can carve a unique pathway to achieving them.

> *Honoring voice and choice in your crew has the potential to unleash creativity and talent you didn't even know existed within your staff.*

Honoring voice and choice in your crew takes the handcuffs off and has the potential to unleash creativity and talent you didn't even know existed within your staff. So in every conversation you have with people about teaching and learning, listen for the opportunities to say, "Go for it!" Support their choices. Let them tell you what they want to try next and follow it up with a "Wow! I'd love to see that! I'm guessing it will make a huge impact on your students. Let me know when you're going to try it because I would love to stop by and see how it goes! Maybe we can even snap a few pictures and Tweet them with our hashtag so everyone can see the impact!"

A Few Cannonballs to Avoid

- Don't honor only the choices you like and the voices you are interested in hearing. Be open to ideas that are different from your own.

- Don't say you support a choice when you really don't. If someone makes a choice you can't get behind, be clear up front and be prepared to share your reasons why.

HONOR VOICE AND CHOICE CHALLENGE

- Reflect: How might your "rulebook" be handicapping your crew?
- Look for ways to allow for teacher voice and choice:

  1. Identify a teacher who has shown an interest in trying something new in his/her classroom from your collaborative conversation last week.

  2. Honor the teacher's voice and choice by being supportive of the idea.

 Share your thoughts, ideas, and artifacts with the *Lead Like a PIRATE* community using the #LeadLAP hashtag.

O is for Offer Support.

We rise by lifting others.

—Robert Ingersoll

Offering support should flow easily after either a collaborative conversation or a captain-directed conversation. When a teacher shares with you something new they want to try or decides to take a risk and push outside their comfort zone, acknowledge that it can sometimes be a challenge or be uncomfortable and then ask, "How can I help?"

We want to be a go-to resource for our crew members. We want them to ask for help when they truly need it, and we want them to know that we support risk taking, learning, and growth and that we will do what we can to get obstacles out of their way and help brainstorm solutions to challenges that arise.

We want our crew to know that it's not perfection but continuous steps toward improvement that we value most.

We want our crew to know that it's not perfection but continuous steps toward improvement that we value most. Not being perfect at something is part of the learning process. The messages administrators give too often convey an expectation of perfection. We can't forget that it takes time to get good at anything worthwhile. Rather than point out faults (which the teacher is likely already aware of), celebrate the fact that the teacher took a chance! Point out what went right, engage in a collaborative conversation about what's next, and then offer support. That may mean providing additional professional development opportunities, but it may be as simple as building in practice time.

A Few Cannonballs to Avoid

- Don't offer support you can't actually provide.
- Don't be a flake. If you commit to a particular support, follow through.

Offer Support Challenge

Offer your support and, of course, your PIRATE enthusiasm for the anticipation of what positive effect the teacher's new practice or skill could have on student learning. It's amazing how an idea mixed with the right amount of enthusiasm can literally cause a learning explosion!

Be sure that you also honor the voice and choice of what support is needed. Most often, the support needed is an extra set of eyes in the classroom, a listening ear, a brainstorm buddy, or simply the right resource. Just don't steamroll the teacher with your ideas. Instead, make sure they know you are there to support them.

Find three ways you can offer support to staff who are trying new things. Who in your system is struggling? Who is looking to take a leap and try something new and innovative? How can you provide or get them (it doesn't always have to be you) the extra support they need?

 Share your thoughts, ideas, and artifacts with the *Lead Like a PIRATE* community using the #LeadLAP hashtag.

R is for Reflection.

Follow effective action with quiet reflection. From the quiet reflection will come even more effective action.
—Peter Drucker

This piece is for you—the leader. At the end of every ANCHOR conversation, take a moment to reflect on how it went. Go back to the three goals outlined at the beginning of this chapter. Ask yourself:

- "Did the teacher walk away knowing that I value her?"
- "Did the teacher find value in my contribution to the conversation?"
- "Did my conversation with him push his thinking, and will it help push practice forward?"

If you answered with a hearty "yes," that is great, but more importantly, what were the intentional actions you took to make a positive impact with the ANCHOR conversation? Those are the things that we want to be sure we keep doing as we continue our work with other coaching conversations.

On the other hand, if you answered with a wishy-washy "yes," or even a "no," what contributed to that answer? What was missing? Once you pinpoint the specific cannonball that snuck into your conversation, first of all, how could you potentially revisit the conversation and how will you adjust your sails for the next person you meet? A critical component of leadership is building in the time and space for honest self-reflection. Without a constant and never-ending drive to improve our own capacity to lead, positive change will stagnate. And to be completely honest, as leaders, we so often rob ourselves of this much-needed time to stop, slow down, and improve our own practice.

 Share your thoughts, ideas, and artifacts with the *Lead Like a PIRATE* community using the #LeadLAP hashtag.

THE POWER OF WORDS

Words are manifested leadership. They have the power to open doors, build bridges, inspire vision, and change the world.
—James Sartain, blog, March 2, 2014

Remember the old adage "Sticks and stones will break my bones, but words will never hurt me"? We beg to differ. Words have power—*a lot* of power. The words we use as leaders matter. People pay attention to them. People make decisions based on them. People go home from work uplifted or beaten down because of them. Even words we say that seem insignificant to us may have a more powerful impact (positive or negative) on someone than we will ever know. So choose your words wisely. Once they are out in the world, you can't take them back—ever.

I (Shelley) have always been a student of words—their power, their impact, their influence. As a leader, I choose what I say and how I say it very purposefully and thoughtfully because I want people to hear and understand my message in the way I intend. I have learned so many excellent lessons about words, their power, and the critical importance of good communication, and I have shared a few of those word treasures in the following pages.

1. As leaders, we have lost the luxury of thinking out loud!

Like it or not, it's true. Even if you define yourself as a highly collaborative leader or a servant leader (or any other kind of leader), you still don't have the luxury of thinking aloud. By the time words come out of your mouth, you need to have thought them through.

As a new principal, I learned early on that once I spoke or shared a thought, others could clam up and be less likely to share their thoughts and ideas. Apparently, once I had spoken and shared my initial thoughts, they assumed the decision had been made and their ideas didn't matter. That is the opposite of who I am or want to be as a leader. In my first year as a principal, I adopted a strategy that I have used on many occasions since. Instead of being the first to talk, I am the last to talk. Instead of sharing, I pose questions—very carefully planned and crafted questions—and then I listen to the other voices in the room. When everyone else has finished sharing, I take on the role of summarizer and synthesizer. Only then do I add my idea if it hasn't already been shared by someone else. Strategies like this one have been essential for me because I genuinely believe that all of those other voices matter. With lots of ideas, we can build one or two amazing ideas to carry us forward, but as soon as I start to think out loud, I run the risk of stifling those other voices.

> *As a leader, as soon as I start to think out loud, I run the risk of stifling those other voices.*

I share the following story with every new leader I have the opportunity to coach. It comes from a principal I used to work with who had an *aha* moment in his first year as a principal. He was freely sharing with one of his teachers several ideas and practices he had just learned about at a PD session he had attended. He was talking to one of his teachers (who used to be a teacher colleague of his) and thinking out loud with her about the kinds of things he had learned and how they might be good for the school. By his account, he stopped mid-sentence when he noticed the teacher's eyes getting wide and her face was turning a little bit green. She was overwhelmed by all that he was saying and the impact all those potential changes would have on her. I'm sure her mind was going a mile a minute about all she would have to do. His reflection with me about that moment was that he suddenly realized that while he was just chattering away in his excitement about things he had learned, she was staring at the giant red stamp on his forehead that only she could see. It read: BOSS. And, to her, every new idea he mentioned wasn't simply an idea, but a mandate that might overload her already-full plate.

As leaders, we need to be heard; people need to know who we are and what we stand for. They need to know what to expect from us and be able to predict how we will respond to a variety of situations. If we always just say the first thing that pops into our heads at any given moment, we can run the risk of diluting our message and creating confusion for people who count on us to stay focused and consistent.

2. Find alternatives for loaded words and phrases.

If you want your message to have maximum impact, pay close attention to how people respond when you use certain words and phrases. Do your words uplift and inspire? Do they set off triggers and cause negative reactions? We want our words to influence and inspire great work. We want the words, phrases, and tones we use to convey to people that we are all part of the same team moving forward together. We want our words to reflect that we value and believe in each person as a professional. We want the words we use to motivate people to try new things, take risks—and feel safe doing so. Because we don't want our words to turn people off, we are as intentional about our word choices as we are the ideas we use them to convey.

For example, I (Shelley) no longer use the word "rigor" when I talk with educators or facilitate professional learning opportunities. It's too loaded. Let me be clear: I truly love the concept that most people are trying to communicate when they use that word, but I don't use it anymore. I've used it often enough in the past, but too many people are turned off by it. They aren't necessarily turned off by the concept it is intended to convey in education, but they are turned off by the word. I have watched people sneer and roll their eyes when it gets used in PD, and I've read numerous blog posts about the horrors of the word (including one written by my husband @burgessdave). So I made a deliberate decision to take it out of my vocabulary when interacting with educators.

Depending on the context and the conversation, I now use phrases like "level of complexity," "complex thinking," "challenging and thought-provoking work," "asking a meaty question that allows for divergent thinking." Phrases like these allow me to communicate the intended concept without evoking the negative reactions I received when I used the word "rigor."

3. Remove judgment language from your feedback.

People don't like to be judged. I know I don't. But I love feedback. I love reflecting with people. I love being challenged and pushed to be better. But judgment? No thanks!

I have supported and coached many educational leaders, instructional coaches, and teacher leaders over the years, and I know removing judgment language from feedback is a challenging but essential practice for all leaders. It's difficult because we are all so prone to it. We make assumptions and pass judgment all the time, even when we don't realize we are doing it.

To get good at eliminating judgment, you have to notice when you are doing it. That means paying attention to the common "judgment phrases" in your daily conversations and replacing them with new language that is void of judgment. Look at the list of a few common phrases administrators use. Do you use any of these?

"I really didn't like the way he ..."

"I just wish she would have ..."

"That's not the way I would have …"

"If only she …"

"What was he thinking?"

These judgments come when we make assumptions and don't take the time to understand the entire situation. One strategy that is particularly helpful to me when I feel that urge to judge someone is to stop and instead ask a question. The question must be genuine, not one of those fake or manipulative questions that people know are judgmental. My rule is that it should be a question that will actually help me understand what's going on. Here is an example:

To know me as an educational leader is to know that I have exceptionally high expectations for students and an unwavering belief in their talents and capabilities. One of the quickest ways to set me off is to tell me that "kids can't." When I walk into a classroom and observe a lesson that appears to be way below grade-level expectations, my first reaction is to judge. Knowing this about myself, I've learned to stop myself before saying something like, "The learning objective you were teaching was way below grade level. What were you *thinking*?" Instead, I stop, take a deep breath, and remind myself my goal is to understand, not judge. I then start the conversation by asking genuine questions in a true attempt to get clarity about what's really going on. My question may sound something like this:

> So when I walked into the room, I noticed you were working with the kids on _____. Tell me more about that lesson and why you chose it as a focus. I'd love to know what made you decide to go there with them.

Over the years, I have received amazing responses to that question. Things I might never have known if my language had put people on the defensive:

> I had just given them a quick pre-assessment on an essential prerequisite skill they needed for the lesson ten minutes before you walked in, and they didn't have it down. To ensure their success I

spent fifteen minutes teaching the essential prerequisite; you should see how they later rocked the lesson.

or

I was reading over their essays last night and noticed a common trend. They just didn't seem to have a grasp on the topic, so we spent some time on it today. Then I had them rewrite their essays, and they were so much better!

When we observe lessons, we can see a lot, but we also have no idea what happened before we walked into the room and no idea what happened after we left. If our assumptions make us quick to judge, we can let judgment language dominate our feedback and conversations. This can quickly close doors to us and rob us of amazing opportunities for incredible dialogue with our teachers, not to mention prevent us from inspiring them to move forward in their practice. If we want to be invited into the real conversations about teaching and learning in our schools, then our teachers need to feel safe and know we aren't judging them.

4. Be careful … most of our praise is judgmental too!

We mentioned in the chapter on ANCHOR conversations that even positive phrases like "Great job!" and "I so loved your lesson on …" are judgmental and cause questions about what we don't love. That's why we advocate for "noticing" language instead. Here's an example of what that may sound like:

Hey, when I was in your classroom today, I noticed that you were trying out a new strategy (insert strategy here). I could tell that it was really making a difference for your kids. When I sat down and talked to Sarah and Johnny, they had real depth in their responses. Sarah said... Johnny said... What were some of the things you noticed? How are you going to expand on that tomorrow? Would you mind if I came by to see that? I expect it will push their learning even further, and I am excited to see where it might go.

Feedback like this is both powerful and perceived as highly positive. It is also void of any judgmental language.

5. Take steps to understand yourself as a communicator.

To be an effective communicator, you first have to understand how others perceive you. A longtime friend of mine recently shared a story about a PD session she had attended in her district. Instead of listening to the message being delivered (which ironically was about the importance of PLCs and teamwork), someone at my friend's table tallied how many times the presenter said the word "I." The number was upward of 175. The presenter, who was a district leader, probably had no idea how often he used the word "I" when communicating to his team, but it was clearly a turn-off to people who were listening; and as a result, his message wasn't heard.

> *To be an effective communicator, you first have to understand how others perceive you.*

Good communicators work on becoming aware of their speaking patterns and habits so they can ensure the real message gets across. So enlist some help! Another longtime friend and principal colleague of mine helped me in this regard. He knew how much words mattered to me, so even when I moved into the assistant superintendent role where I was technically his boss, he helped keep me on my toes with my language. He would catch phrases that I might start to overuse and send me little slips of paper with the phrase and a big "X" drawn through it. He noticed and pointed out "trigger" words that were starting to cause some grumbling among our colleagues. He also helped me understand which words and phrases had made a powerful and positive impact on him. I appreciated every one of these exchanges because they helped me grow and get better.

POWER OF WORDS CHALLENGE

What are words or phrases used in your system that can make people bristle? Create alternatives that still convey your intended message without getting people's hackles up. Use these instead.

 Share your thoughts, ideas, and artifacts with the *Lead Like a PIRATE* community using the #LeadLAP hashtag.

SECTION IV

BE A BETTER CAPTAIN

Leading others well only happens when you first lead yourself well. In this final section we will shine the light on a few of the dangers to watch out for on your journey. We'll also encourage you to strive for authentic greatness. We know you have it in you to be the PIRATE captain your crew deserves.

Go for Greatness

Leaders are fascinated by the future. You are a leader if and only if you are restless for change, impatient for progress, and deeply dissatisfied with status quo. Because in your head, you can see a better future. The friction between "what is" and "what could be" burns you, stirs you up, propels you. This is leadership.
—Marcus Buckingham, *The One Thing You Need to Know*

In any given moment we have two options: to step forward into growth or to step back into safety.
—Abraham Maslow

Do you want to be great? In *Teach Like a PIRATE*, Dave points out that this question is often met with awkward silence. It's not that people don't want to be great; it's that they feel uncomfortable admitting their willingness to be great, as if this desire is somehow selfish or egotistical. Alternatively, they may want to be great, but doubt their ability or may even fear the work required to achieve greatness.

We want you to be great! You are engaged in life-changing work, so mediocrity is not an option. You don't get to be a great leader without rolling up your sleeves and doing the hard work, putting in the work to develop new leaders, and creating opportunities for your team to continuously learn and grow. Greatness requires listening to and learning from those who work with you. It demands that you keep pushing forward in order to meet the changing needs of your school and your students. And, like the quest for success, you never actually arrive at greatness; it's a moving target, a lifelong pursuit. But, if you're willing to do the work, it's a quest that will yield amazing experiences.

In my (Beth's) early days of the principalship, I tended to second -guess my actions and wonder too much about what others might think. I was less bold and more bland in my approach to topics that could cause controversy. Eventually, I realized all that wondering and worrying was keeping me from being the leader I could be, the leader who was needed, the leader I wanted to be.

> ## *You never actually arrive at greatness; it's a moving target, a lifelong pursuit.*

You do have to consider how your words and actions will impact others, but if you play it too safe, you'll never accomplish anything truly great. The reality is, the complainers are going to complain no matter what. So anytime you start to worry about what others will say in response to a tough decision you have to make, think about your best and most respected teachers. They are the ones who will benefit most from your greatness. And they are the ones seeking greatness for your students. It is more important to support those going above and beyond than to pander to those who try to maintain the status quo.

GREATNESS CHALLENGE

- Take a couple of minutes to define what greatness in your position entails. Now spend some time writing down the steps necessary to move toward your vision of greatness.

- Who do you believe models greatness in our profession? What makes it so? Reach out to them. Ask about their challenges and how they moved past those to become great.

- No holds barred: If you could do anything, what would it be? What is holding you back? What is one thing you can do today to move you closer to that goal?

 Share your thoughts, ideas, and artifacts with the *Lead Like a PIRATE* community using the #LeadLAP hashtag.

DEALING WITH CRITICS

He has the right to criticize who has the heart to help.
—Abraham Lincoln

It behooves every man to remember that the work of the critic is of altogether secondary importance, and that, in the end, progress is accomplished by the man who does things.
—Theodore Roosevelt

Although everyone claims to be searching for greatness, many are just searching for comfortable. PIRATE leaders push the envelope each and every day. This makes people uncomfortable. Expect critics.

There are two very different forms of criticism: constructive and destructive. Constructive criticism is offered by people who truly want to help you succeed. The insights that accompany constructive criticism can help make you and your school better and can help you to recalculate if you've gone off course. And although it's easiest to accept criticism from those we trust, it is important to be open to feedback from those who have a stake in the education of our students.

In contrast, destructive criticism is offered with a drastically different intent. The goals of these critics are usually to hurt both the people and the mission of an organization. Sometimes these critics attempt to disguise their input as constructive, but when you analyze their message, it is complaint driven, not solution oriented. These critics can be bullies and tend to cause drama, which completely takes away from the important work we do.

The best way to silence destructive critics is to eliminate them from your life as much as possible. Deal with them like you deal with negative people: have little or nothing to do with them. Unfortunately, there are times when the destructive critic is a coworker or parent with whom you have to interact. They seem to have a problem for every solution.

When faced with these critics, do as Michelle Obama said, "When they go low, we go high." One way you can do this is to strive to always presume positive intentions. If a person is being critical, it could be possible that they don't realize they are being destructive vs. constructive. Look inward before responding to these critics. Have you done a good-enough job of building a compelling "why"? Does the person truly understand what he or she is criticizing? If not, work to build a better understanding of your mission.

But if the answer to those questions is "yes," then challenge the destructive critic in a respectful way. Ask them for examples, goals, vision, solutions that will help solve the problem. Sure, you could sigh loudly or offer a look of total bewilderment at the criticism, but a more effective response is this: "Help me understand what you are talking about." If at all possible, have these kinds of clarifying conversations in person. Emails or social-media conversations do not provide the advantage of tone and body language and can easily lead to misinterpretation. There is absolutely nothing to be gained by engaging in a negative back-and-forth print dialogue. Furthermore, a confrontation is not the kind of thing you want added to your digital footprint.

Try to use social media to your advantage when it comes to critics. For example, I (Beth) have learned to embrace Facebook as a gauge to public opinion. One of my staff members is friends with most everyone in town and lets me know when we have someone upset about our school. I take time to call the parent/community member and ask what I can do to help. Just this small act can defuse what is typically a misunderstanding. Once people know they can speak to you and ask direct questions, the instances of negative posts on social media will decrease. By being available, you build rapport and help eliminate online gossip.

> ## Once people know they can speak to you and ask direct questions, the instances of negative posts on social media will decrease.

If, in fact, people do intend to be destructive, little you can do or say will change their views. Your strength comes from your commitment to continue to grow and do what is best for the people around you. Don't let destructive critics steal the energy that should go into making your school amazing. If you stop listening to the critics, they may eventually stop complaining. If nothing else, you can always block them on social media.

CRITIC CHALLENGE

Who have been the biggest critics in your career? What was their purpose? How did you respond? Next time you are criticized or an initiative you've proposed comes under fire, choose not to flare up and fight back. Instead, ask for understanding: "Help me understand what you're talking about," or ask, "What other ideas do you have to improve our plan?"

 Share your thoughts, ideas, and artifacts with the *Lead Like a PIRATE* community using the #LeadLAP hashtag.

DISCOVER THE POWER OF A PLN

To have thousands of fellow minds in your pocket via mobile devices is to have an immensely unfair advantage over humans who think alone.
—Kevin Honeycutt

Being a connected educator is the single most important thing I've done to transform how I teach. I have gathered and tried new ideas. I've learned, asked questions, and developed an amazing online, professional learning network.
—Matt Miller, *Ditch That Textbook*

One of the biggest shifts I (Beth) struggled with when transitioning from the classroom to the front office was moving from the support of a team of teachers to the solitude of being principal. As leaders, we are entrusted to so much confidential, stressful, and oftentimes heart-wrenching information. In my early years, I struggled to process it all mentally and emotionally. I hit a wall in the summer of 2014, and I considered leaving the profession. The punitive shift education had taken, coupled with the loneliness of leadership, had me in a very bad place. Luckily, a coworker and good friend of mine, Connie Epperson, convinced me to go to a national principal conference and it was just what I needed. I realized two important things at this conference. First, as leaders, we must take time to engage in specific learning opportunities that help to improve our craft. We spend so much time in our positions working to help provide learning and growth to our staff that we forget about developing ourselves specifically in our roles. Secondly, I was introduced to the incredible power of a professional learning network (PLN) to combat the isolation of leadership. Until that moment, I thought Twitter was just another social media tool to keep up with what the celebrities were up to at the moment. PIRATE principal Jay Billy taught me the ins and outs of using Twitter as a tool to connect and gain access to 24/7 free professional development. Wow!

A PLN is one of the most powerful resources you can build for yourself. Social media has knocked down the barriers of time and distance. Today, you can connect with other professionals across the street or around the globe. Your PLN can (and should) consist of other school leaders and educators as well as people who aren't in education. It is also important to connect with people who have similar and contrasting views to your own so that you will be pushed to consider multiple viewpoints and contrasting ideas. A PLN gives you the opportunity to take part in professional learning whenever and wherever you want. It connects you to amazing educators, provides access to resources, and can help you to keep up with the latest trends in education and leadership.

A PLN is one of the most powerful resources you can build for yourself.

Being the organizational leader can be lonely and difficult. With technology, we no longer have to go it alone. We don't have to have every answer to every question. In fact, if you have a question, there's a good chance it has already been asked and the answer is just a few keystrokes, Facebook group, or Twitter or Google search away. By building your

PLN, you can use the brains and experiences of all those brilliant minds out there to guide you and give you support.

PLN Challenge

- Take FIVE!

    1. Find five new educators to add to your PLN.
    2. Find five new tech enthusiasts to add to your PLN.
    3. Find five new leaders outside of education to add to your PLN.
    4. Find five new authors to add to your PLN.
    5. Find five people outside your country to add to your PLN.

- Identify one member of your PLN and thank them for some way that they helped you. Be specific.

- Write a blog post or develop a PD opportunity with someone in your PLN whom you do not see on a daily basis.

 Share your thoughts, ideas, and artifacts with the *Lead Like a PIRATE* community using the #LeadLAP hashtag.

STAY TRUE TO YOUR ROOTS

This above all: to thine own self be true.
—Shakespeare, *Hamlet*

uilding- and district-level leadership requires you to wear many hats, but we both agree that there is one hat that we can never take off: the teacher hat. If you are a leader, you can't ever forget what it is like to be in a classroom. The best way to do this is to set aside time to teach occasionally. Of course, you can't spend all of your time teaching and forget about your responsibilities as a leader, but there are many ways to keep your foot in the classroom and walk the talk of what you expect from your staff.

One of the things I (Beth) love the most about being a principal is the variety and uncertainty each day brings. I begin to receive the daily substitute reports at 5:30 a.m. I remember one particular day that did not look promising. We were three subs short and had no one available to call. By the time I got to school, it was evident that I would be the substitute for one of our classes. I had a full list of things I needed to do, and at first, I wasn't too excited about getting further behind. But then

I thought, *What could be better than spending a whole day with second graders?*

I put on my principal coat to do morning duty and the word was already out on the street! Kids looked a little worried and parents had big smiles on their faces. Teachers reminded me to go to the bathroom now while I had the chance. I shifted into teacher mode when the bell rang and headed to the classroom. I had already taken time to drop off my bag of tricks and treats.

This hook awaited them on the whiteboard as they walked in . . .

GOOD MORNING!
ENTER . . . IF YOU DARE!
YOUR TEACHER HAS BEEN KIDNAPPED!
BE READY! WE ARE GOING TO BE LEARNING PIRATE TRICKS!
BUT SHHHHH! DON'T TELL ANYONE!

Class started with a buzz of energy as kids tried to figure out where the teacher could be and dealt with the shock of having the principal as their substitute. I used this to my advantage as I introduced the first step of being a PIRATE to the kids: Passion. We met together for a "Hornet Huddle" class meeting, and I asked the kids to think about what they were most passionate about. I wanted to do a little team building and have a chance to figure out how I could better teach them throughout my time in their classroom. It was so great to hear all of the different passions the kids expressed, from reading to football to music and math. I also shared my passions with the kids. They loved to hear about my passion for learning, books, Hawaii, and exercise.

We finished up our huddle and were off to specials. Before they left, I gave them another teaser about what may be happening when they returned to the classroom. I wanted to be sure that if given a choice, the kids would *want* to be in the classroom with me.

Whew! The morning was a blur as we did more team-building activities and reading. I sat and listened to each student read and then asked them questions to check comprehension. We also did some very fun vocabulary activities to learn our words through movement. I can guarantee you that everyone in our class definitely understood what *vote* and *wait* meant!

Before we knew it, it was time for lunch. We took a minute to stretch out and do a brain boost before we ate. "Wipeout" was the song that won the vote and we showed off our dance moves. Heads cleared and stomachs growling, we were off to lunch!

I scarfed down my food and a little more caffeine, and I was back at it ready to go! First, a read-aloud with a special book from Hawaii, then time for math—and I could tell it was going to be a tough sell. The after-lunch nap attack had hit the kids. So we got moving. We counted like pirates, we added like pirates, we made ballpark estimates like pirates, we moved and danced and sang until we truly understood the math concepts. The best comment from this time of the day was, "Wow, Mrs. Houf, you are like a real teacher!" *Priceless.*

The remainder of the day was filled with writing creative stories about why their teacher wasn't at school and sharing out with their peers. They gave specific feedback to one another and made revisions and were ready and excited to showcase their creativity with their teacher when she returned.

However, one of our class pirates wasn't so excited to share his creativity. A bout of writer's block had him very upset. His frustration provided the perfect opportunity segue into our final activity of the day, The Power of Yet.

This was one that I brought in myself, taking advantage of a teachable moment. Kids (and adults for that matter) seem to think that everything has to be perfect on the first try. Two attributes our school wanted to promote that year were risk taking and "thinking outside the box." Students took time to write down three things that they can't do . . . yet, and we put together a short video to inspire others to remember the power of yet (bit.ly/McYET).

What an amazing day! It made me realize the importance of school leaders staying involved and engaged in all that is expected of our classroom teachers. Every principal, and district leader for that matter, should take time periodically to sub one full day in a classroom. It keeps you grounded, reminds you to stay current in teaching practices and classroom-management strategies, and helps build relationships with students. It was an exhilarating, exhausting, engaging day for this guest teacher. I truly tried to provide an uncommon experience for the students I was lucky enough to teach and was definitely rewarded with uncommon effort and attitude.

The transition from the classroom to another position in a school can be awkward. But even as PIRATE teachers shift into PIRATE leaders, they stay connected to the heartbeat of the classroom. What do you do when you are short on subs? Do you divide kids and make other classes bigger? Do you pull other staff to cover? How often do you roll your sleeves up and cover classes to ensure that learning is still the number-one focus? It is one thing to say you value servant leadership; it is another to make it happen.

STAY TRUE TO YOUR ROOTS CHALLENGE

- How can you find time to get in the classroom without neglecting your daily leadership tasks? How could you commit to being the "mystery teacher" one period a week (or a month, start somewhere) to allow the classroom teacher to collaborate with colleagues or observe others?

- Create a monthly or quarterly drawing where the winner gets to spend the day developing lessons and materials while you teach their class. Part of the day, the winner gets to observe you and give feedback.

Share your thoughts, ideas, and artifacts with the *Lead Like a PIRATE* community using the #LeadLAP hashtag.

Knowing When
to Take the
Leadership Leap

Faith is taking the first step, even when you can't see the whole staircase.
—Dr. Martin Luther King Jr.

Amazing things happen in your un-comfort zone.
—Beth Houf

We must be willing to let go of the life we have planned, so as to have the life that is waiting for us.
—Joseph Campbell

A ship is always safe at shore, but that is not what it is built for.
—Albert Einstein

One of the most frequent questions that Shelley and I get asked is how we knew it was time to make the move from the classroom to other leadership positions. What was that deciding factor to making the shift? The answer to that question is never simple, but there are definitely common signs that it is time to take the leadership leap. As hard as this may be to believe, I never wanted to be a principal. I loved teaching and the opportunity it gave me to impact students in the classroom. The energy from students was contagious, and it was a catalyst for creativity as I planned lessons. I truly thought I would retire as a classroom teacher.

Missouri's State Department of Education had a unique program for classroom teachers called STARR (Select Teachers as Regional Resources). Looking for a challenge, I applied and was one of the two selected from our region for a two-year period. During this time, I was deeply engaged in professional development taught by some of the nation's greatest educators. In the second year of this program, I was on sabbatical from my classroom and provided professional development (organized through our regional professional-development center) to forty area schools on a variety of topics. Throughout this year of working with schools, one overwhelming fact hit me like a ton of bricks: The highest-functioning schools had the highest-functioning leaders. Don't get me wrong. I know and wholeheartedly believe the research that shows that the classroom teacher is the greatest factor in student learning. But I quickly realized that these teachers, overall, do not like to work for leaders who are ineffective. Not only do they not like to work with them, they flock in exodus from them as soon as they can! So many times, I left schools frustrated because the teachers there were ready to move forward, and the leader was holding them back. I was in an awkward position because I felt as though it wasn't my place to criticize and offer leadership suggestions.

How will you know when you are ready to take a leadership leap?

It was a year of tremendous growth for me as an educator, but also a time that I began to question my career trajectory. I loved teaching, but I realized I had a passion for supporting teachers through professional development. I loved the change that I could help to facilitate with a class of students, but I realized that if I really wanted to make lasting impact, change needed to happen on a larger scale. I wrestled with this discomfort and was looking for a sign of what to do next. Meanwhile, I was perfectly happy with the idea of returning to the classroom the next year. Or was I?

That winter, I was at a local mall doing some holiday shopping. I happened to run into a teacher in my home district where there was an elementary principal opening. She told me that I needed to consider applying for this position. She saw something in me that I didn't know was there. The "sign" I had been waiting for showed up, but I still wasn't sure what I wanted to do. *Do I stay or do I go? Is this the right move for me? Could I really be a principal? Was I ready to leave the classroom?* After much reflection and conversation with family and friends, t-charts of pros and cons, and sleepless nights, I decided to apply for the position. My tipping-point moment came when I realized that I had to be okay with the possibility of not being selected. I wholeheartedly could say that this was the case. I was ready to push my un-comfort zone with the idea of a new leadership challenge, but I was perfectly happy returning to the classroom.

The next seven years I had the privilege of being the principal of McIntire Elementary. I learned so much from the experiences and opportunities. I grew in more ways than I ever thought possible. I am eternally grateful to the McIntire staff for teaching me more about leadership than I could read in any book or learn in college classes. Each person taught me in his or her own way how to strive for greatness. They taught me that it is all about our kids, but we can't forget to support each other. They taught me that a leader has to take risks and model what is expected for staff and students. They taught me that there are no excuses when striving to meet goals, no matter the roadblocks. They taught me that a leader takes people where they need to go, which is not always where they want to go. They taught me to lead not only with my head, but also my heart. They taught me that we truly can build a school where students, educators, and parents want to run in and not out. They taught me that we must celebrate our students and one another every day. They taught me that, when we put our focus on raising human potential, better test scores will result—and to never mix up the emphasis. Most importantly, they taught me that amazing things happen in our un-comfort zones.

They taught me all of this and so much more, and for this, I will always be thankful. I loved being the principal of McIntire Elementary. I found joy in my profession and couldn't imagine doing anything else. Or so I thought.

On an early Friday evening in January of 2015, my superintendent called and asked if I had a moment to talk. My natural instinct was to immediately wonder what I had done wrong or who I might have offended. He came into my office, and I knew something was different. He then asked if I would consider moving to the open principal position at our local middle school. I worked really hard to control the contortion of my face. Middle school? Was he serious? Middle school was the most difficult time of my life; why would I want to return? At the time, I was dealing with some pretty scary health issues. Also, I loved my school. Immediately, I told him thank you so much for considering me but that I was really not interested in moving at the moment.

As soon as he left my office, the feeling I'd had seven years earlier returned. I couldn't stop thinking about that meeting. I wondered if I had answered correctly. Our district had a need. This need impacted me deeply professionally and personally, as my oldest would move to the middle school in six short months. Was I being selfish by staying in my comfort zone? A couple months later, I was asked again to consider moving to the middle school. This time my answer was yes. It was one of the hardest decisions I had ever made, but a peace settled over me knowing that it may not be what I had planned, but it was what was needed.

With the decision made, I had to face my current staff and students. We had a staff meeting immediately so they could hear it from me first. I am not an overly emotional person, but the tears were impossible to hold back. We were a team and a family. We had dedicated the past seven years to developing and truly living out our mission, vision, and collective commitments. We'd overcome failure and roadblocks by rising out of school improvement status due to our tireless efforts. We had said goodbye to two students who left this earth way too early. We had celebrated weddings, babies, and family milestones together. We had built a student-centered professional learning community. We had grown and learned so much together. We had found comfort in our un-comfort zones. Then I thought back to seven years prior and remembered the same bittersweet feelings I had when saying goodbye to a classroom of students and amazing colleagues. As hard as it was to make the move, it was the right decision. I knew this decision, too, was right.

During the past two years at Fulton Middle School, I have found another home and family. I work with amazing educators who strive to make a lifelong impact for students at what we hope is the best middle school ever. I have the opportunity to interact with every single student in our school system. How amazing is that? Although the change and move have had their share of highs and lows, it was the leadership leap that needed to happen—to help our district, our students, and to stretch my leadership skills.

Are you pondering a leadership leap but just aren't sure if you are ready? Every situation is completely different, but there are a few key questions to consider:

- What is the purpose for your wanting to make the move? Is it time to push your comfort zone for a new challenge? Are you yearning for a chance to lead?

- Would you be moving to a situation that matches your passion and work style? For example, if you want complete freedom to make site-level decisions, would you be able to work in a district that expects all leaders throughout the system to make collaborative district-wide procedures? If you are passionate about risk taking and innovation, how well would you fit with a district that is more traditional in its instructional delivery model?

- Are the new responsibilities of the career change worth the additional salary you may earn? Does your new position require nightly sports and extracurricular-activity supervision? When you divide the additional income earned by the additional hours worked, what do you notice?

- Are you only making the shift to move up the ladder or for more money? This is a plank walker for sure. If money or title is the only reason for a leadership leap, you are making the wrong decision. Period. Those who go into leadership for these reasons are the ones who tend to give school leaders a bad rap.

- What type of support system do you have both in the educational setting and personally? Career changes are hard. The support is imperative for both the physical and emotional toll it takes on a person.

- What is your intuition telling you? Are there warning signs that keep popping into your mind? Are you excited at the possibility of the change?

The positive thing to always remember is that you have a large support system within this PLN that is ready to help you lead like a PIRATE! Are you ready to take the leap?

Take the Leap Challenge

Spend some time identifying your long-term career plans in education. What would you like to be doing next year? 3 years from now? 5? 10? Are you on the right path? If not, what could you start to do NOW that helps you get back on course?

Share your thoughts, ideas, and artifacts with the *Lead Like a PIRATE* community using the #LeadLAP hashtag.

REST ... LIKE A PIRATE

Given the stressors of modern American education, it is crucial that we, especially as educators, have a place to retreat to where we access and develop that sense of calm and equanimity that allows us to regroup and come back to our work-a-day lives refreshed and ready to go another round with the challenges life throws at us.

—"The Importance of Sanctuaries" blog post
by Dan Tricarico, author of *The Zen Teacher*

We PIRATE types tend to never stop. Our bodies and brains are constantly on the go. It takes a lot of energy to lead like a PIRATE. As we near the end of the book, take a moment to reflect on how well you take time to rest and recharge. We challenge you to invest time in yourself. Renew your energy using one or more of the following activities and tell us about it on Twitter using the #LeadLAP hashtag.

P is for Passion: What is something you are personally passionate about? Your family? A hobby? Devote time to your personal passions each week.

I is for Immersion: Immerse yourself in you! This may sound selfish, but take time for you instead of giving it all to others. Get that massage you've been putting off. Go watch a movie you've wanted to see.

R is for Rapport: Connect with a family member or friend you've been missing. Take time to build rapport with someone you've neglected. And hey, it's okay if that person is you.

A is for Ask and Analyze: Make a conscious effort to ask yourself each day if you've taken a few moments for you. Analyze the impact of what even five minutes of refocusing does for your practice.

T is for Transformation: How can you transform your current schedule to allow for more time for recharging, relaxing, and resting so you can be more effective as a leader? If you haven't read *The Zen Teacher* by #ZenTeacher Dan Tricarico, it may be a good place to get ideas (bit.ly/ZenTeacher).

E is for Enthusiasm: How can you bring more enthusiasm to your life outside of school? This is a very personal goal for me (Beth). This past school year especially has required much longer hours at school. My own two boys tend to get what is left of me instead of the best of me. That has to change. They deserve as much if not more of my enthusiasm each and every day. For me, this means I am going to need to do a better job of eating right and exercising, which always brings up my energy levels!

Leading like a PIRATE can be exhausting. Taking time to rest is imperative to truly be your best you! Unfortunately, the first things we tend to cut out of our schedule when things get busy are sleep, exercise, and our own passions.

REST CHALLENGE

Be intentional about your PIRATE life. Schedule time for yourself on your calendar. Make resting like a PIRATE a priority so that you can truly *Lead* like a PIRATE.

 Share your thoughts, ideas, and artifacts with the *Lead Like a PIRATE* community using the #LeadLAP hashtag.

CALL TO ACTION

In this book, we've shared our stories, ideas, and beliefs about what it means to be a PIRATE leader. We've shared the trials and tribulations of being a school or district leader in this era where testing and standardization have drilled into our creativity and innovation. Mostly, we hope that we shared how amazing it can be to serve as a leader and the power you have to change lives forever.

As a leader, you not only have a responsibility to serve the students in your school, but you also have an obligation to support the teachers who are in the trenches every day. It is your responsibility to give them the tools they need to do their jobs and remove the roadblocks so that the amazing can happen. We are here for you and happy to support you on your journey. Reach out on Twitter at @burgess_shelley or @BethHouf or by using our hashtag #LeadLAP. You can also find all of our contact information and other *Lead Like a PIRATE* resources on our website leadlikeapirate.net.

Model what you hope for in your teachers and your students. Take risks, try new things, and don't be afraid to have fun doing it. Build a school or a district where students, staff, and families are running to get in rather than out. You can do it! Make it happen! ***Lead Like A Pirate!***

Notes

Chapter 1
Wiseman, Liz, L. Allen, E. Foster. *The Multiplier Effect: Tapping the Genius Inside Our Schools*. Corwin, 2013.

Chapter 3
Jimmy Casas, "Check Boxes: 8 Things We Need to Uncheck," *Passion, Purpose, Pride*. June 17, 2016, http://www.jimmycasas.com/check-boxes-8-things-we-need-to-uncheck.

Chapter 4
Maxwell, John C. *Good Leaders Ask Great Questions*. Center Street a division of Hachette Book Group, 2014.

Chapter 8
Wooden, John and Steve Jamison. *Coach Wooden's Leadership Game Plan for Success: 12 Lessons for Extraordinary Performance and Personal Excellence*. McGraw-Hill Education, 2009.

Chapter 13
Calkins, Lucy, M. Ehrenworth, and C. Lehman. *Pathways to the Common Core: Accelerating Achievement*. Heinemann, 2012.

Sinek, Simon. *Start with Why*. Portfolio, 2009.

Dave Burgess Consulting, Inc.

Teach Like a PIRATE

Increase Student Engagement, Boost Your Creativity, and Transform Your Life as an Educator
By Dave Burgess (@BurgessDave)

Teach Like a PIRATE is the *New York Times'* best-selling book that has sparked a worldwide educational revolution. It is part inspirational manifesto that ignites passion for the profession, and part practical road map filled with dynamic strategies to dramatically increase student engagement. Translated into multiple languages, its message resonates with educators who want to design outrageously creative lessons and transform school into a life-changing experience for students.

P is for PIRATE

Inspirational ABC's for Educators
By Dave and Shelley Burgess
(@Burgess_Shelley)

Teaching is an adventure that stretches the imagination and calls for creativity every day! In *P is for PIRATE*, husband and wife team Dave and Shelley Burgess encourage and inspire educators to make their classrooms fun and exciting places to learn. Tapping into years of personal experience and drawing on the insights of more than seventy educators, the authors offer a wealth of ideas for making learning and teaching more fulfilling than ever before.

Learn Like a PIRATE

Empower Your Students to
Collaborate, Lead, and Succeed
By Paul Solarz (@PaulSolarz)

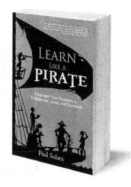

Today's job market demands that students be prepared to take responsibility for their lives and careers. We do them a disservice if we teach them how to earn passing grades without equipping them to take charge of their education. In *Learn Like a PIRATE*, Paul Solarz explains how to design classroom experiences that encourage students to take risks and explore their passions in a stimulating, motivating, and supportive environment where improvement, rather than grades, is the focus. Discover how student-led classrooms help students thrive and develop into self-directed, confident citizens who are capable of making smart, responsible decisions, all on their own.

Play Like a Pirate

Engage Students with Toys, Games, and Comics
By Quinn Rollins (@jedikermit)

Yes! Serious learning can be seriously fun. In *Play Like a Pirate*, Quinn Rollins offers practical, engaging strategies and resources that make it easy to integrate fun into your curriculum. Regardless of the grade level you teach, you'll find inspiration and ideas that will help you engage your students in unforgettable ways.

eXPlore Like a Pirate

*Gamification and Game-Inspired Course Design
to Engage, Enrich, and Elevate Your Learners*
By Michael Matera (@MrMatera)

Are you ready to transform your classroom into an experiential world that flourishes
on collaboration and creativity? Then set sail
with classroom game designer and educator
Michael Matera as he reveals the possibilities
and power of game-based learning. In *eXPlore
Like a Pirate*, Matera serves as your experienced guide to help you apply
the most motivational techniques of game play to your classroom. You'll
learn gamification strategies that will work with and enhance (rather than
replace) your current curriculum and discover how these engaging methods can be applied to any grade level or subject.

Pure Genius

*Building a Culture of Innovation and
Taking 20% Time to the Next Level*
By Don Wettrick (@DonWettrick)

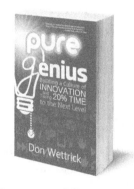

For far too long, schools have been bas-
tions of boredom, killers of creativity, and
way too comfortable with compliance and
conformity. In *Pure Genius*, Don Wettrick
explains how collaboration—with experts,
students, and other educators—can help
you create interesting, and even life-changing, opportunities for learning.
Wettrick's book inspires and equips educators with a systematic blueprint
for teaching innovation in any school.

The Innovator's Mindset

Empower Learning, Unleash Talent, and Lead a Culture of Creativity

By George Couros (@gcouros)

The traditional system of education requires students to hold their questions and compliantly stick to the scheduled curriculum. But our job as educators is to provide new and better opportunities for our students. It's time to recognize that compliance doesn't foster innovation, encourage critical thinking, or inspire creativity—and those are the skills our students need to succeed. In *The Innovator's Mindset*, George Couros encourages teachers and administrators to empower their learners to wonder, to explore—and to become forward-thinking leaders.

Ditch That Textbook

Free Your Teaching and Revolutionize Your Classroom

By Matt Miller (@jmattmiller)

Textbooks are symbols of centuries of old education. They're often outdated as soon as they hit students' desks. Acting "by the textbook" implies compliance and a lack of creativity. It's time to ditch those textbooks—and those textbook assumptions about learning! In *Ditch That Textbook*, teacher and blogger Matt Miller encourages educators to throw out meaningless, pedestrian teaching and learning practices. He empowers them to evolve and improve on old, standard teaching methods. *Ditch That Textbook* is a support system, toolbox, and manifesto to help educators free their teaching and revolutionize their classrooms.

LAUNCH

*Using Design Thinking to Boost Creativity and
Bring Out the Maker in Every Student*
By John Spencer and A.J. Juliani
(@spencerideas, @ajjuliani)

Something happens in students when
they define themselves as makers and inventors and creators. They discover powerful
skills—problem solving, critical thinking,
and imagination—that will help them shape the world's future ... our
future. In *LAUNCH*, John Spencer and A.J. Juliani provide a process
that can be incorporated into every class at every grade level ... even
if you don't consider yourself a "creative teacher." And if you dare to
innovate and view creativity as an essential skill, you will empower
your students to change the world—starting right now.

Master the Media

*How Teaching Media Literacy Can Save Our
Plugged-in World*
By Julie Smith

Written to help teachers and parents educate the next generation, *Master the Media*
explains the history, purpose, and messages
behind the media. The point isn't to get kids
to unplug; it's to help them make informed
choices, understand the difference between
truth and lies, and discern perception from reality. Critical thinking leads
to smarter decisions—and it's why media literacy can save the world.

50 Things You Can Do with Google Classroom

By Alice Keeler and Libbi Miller

It can be challenging to add new technology to the classroom, but it's a must if students are going to be well-equipped for the future. Alice Keeler and Libbi Miller shorten the learning curve by providing a thorough overview of the Google Classroom App. Part of Google Apps for Education (GAfE), Google Classroom was specifically designed to help teachers save time by streamlining the process of going digital. Complete with screenshots, *50 Things You Can Do with Google Classroom* provides ideas and step-by-step instructions to help teachers implement this powerful tool.

50 Things to Go Further with Google Classroom

A Student-Centered Approach

By Alice Keeler and Libbi Miller

(@alicekeeler, @MillerLibbi)

Today's technology empowers educators to move away from the traditional classroom where teachers lead and students work independently—each doing the same thing. In *50 Things to Go Further with Google Classroom: A Student-Centered Approach*, authors and educators Alice Keeler and Libbi Miller offer inspiration and resources to help you create a digitally rich, engaging, student-centered environment. They show you how to tap into the power of individualized learning that is possible with Google Classroom.

140 Twitter Tips for Educators

Get Connected, Grow Your Professional Learning
Network, and Reinvigorate Your Career
By Brad Currie, Billy Krakower, and Scott Rocco
(@bradmcurrie, @wkrakower,
@ScottRRocco)

Whatever questions you have about education
or about how you can be even better at your job,
you'll find ideas, resources, and a vibrant network of professionals ready
to help you on Twitter. In *140 Twitter Tips for Educators,* #Satchat hosts
and founders of Evolving Educators, Brad Currie, Billy Krakower, and
Scott Rocco offer step-by-step instructions to help you master the basics
of Twitter, build an online following, and become a Twitter rock star.

Your School Rocks ... So Tell People!

Passionately Pitch and Promote the Positives
Happening on Your Campus
By Ryan McLane and Eric Lowe
(@McLane_Ryan, @EricLowe21)

Great things are happening in your school
every day. The problem is, no one beyond your
school walls knows about them. School principals
Ryan McLane and Eric Lowe want to help you
get the word out! In *Your School Rocks ... So Tell*
People! McLane and Lowe offer more than seventy immediately actionable tips along with easy-to-follow instructions and links to video tutori-
als. This practical guide will equip you to create an effective and manage-
able communication strategy using social-media tools. Learn how to keep
your students' families and community connected, informed, and excited
about what's going on in your school.

The Zen Teacher

Creating FOCUS, SIMPLICITY, and
TRANQUILITY in the Classroom
By Dan Tricarico (@thezenteacher)

Teachers have incredible power to influence, even improve, the future. In *The Zen Teacher,* educator, blogger, and speaker Dan Tricarico provides practical, easy-to-use techniques to help teachers be their best—unrushed and fully focused—so they can maximize their performance and improve their quality of life. In this introductory guide, Dan Tricarico explains what it means to develop a Zen practice—something that has nothing to do with religion and everything to do with your ability to thrive in the classroom.

The Classroom Chef

Sharpen your lessons. Season your classes. Make
math meaningful.
By John Stevens and Matt Vaudrey
(@Jstevens009, @MrVaudrey)

In *The Classroom Chef,* math teachers and instructional coaches John Stevens and Matt Vaudrey share their secret recipes, ingredients, and tips for serving up lessons that engage students and help them "get" math. You can use these ideas and methods as-is, or better yet, tweak them and create your own enticing educational meals. The message the authors share is that, with imagination and preparation, every teacher can be a Classroom Chef.

How Much Water Do We Have?

5 Success Principles for Conquering Any Change and Thriving in Times of Change
By Pete Nunweiler with Kris Nunweiler

In *How Much Water Do We Have?* Pete Nunweiler identifies five key elements—information, planning, motivation, support, and leadership—that are necessary for the success of any goal, life transition, or challenge. Referring to these elements as the 5 Waters of Success, Pete explains that, like the water we drink, you need them to thrive in today's rapidly paced world. If you're feeling stressed out, overwhelmed, or uncertain at work or at home, pause and look for the signs of dehydration. Learn how to find, acquire, and use the 5 Waters of Success—so you can share them with your team and family members.

The Writing on the Classroom Wall

How Posting Your Most Passionate Beliefs about Education Can Empower Your Students, Propel Your Growth, and Lead to a Lifetime of Learning
By Steve Wyborney (@SteveWyborney)

In *The Writing on the Classroom Wall*, Steve Wyborney explains how posting and discussing Big Ideas can lead to deeper learning. You'll learn why sharing your ideas will sharpen and refine them. You'll also be encouraged to know that the Big Ideas you share don't have to be profound to make a profound impact on learning. In fact, Steve explains, it's okay if some of your ideas fall off the wall. What matters most is sharing them.

Kids Deserve It!

Pushing Boundaries and Challenging
Conventional Thinking
By Todd Nesloney and Adam Welcome
(@TechNinjaTodd, @awelcome)

In *Kids Deserve It!*, Todd and Adam encourage you to think big and make learning fun and meaningful for students. Their high-tech, high-touch, and highly engaging practices will inspire you to take risks, shake up the status quo, and be a champion for your students. While you're at it, you just might rediscover why you became an educator in the first place.

Instant Relevance

Using Today's Experiences in
Tomorrow's Lessons
By Denis Sheeran (@MathDenisNJ)

Every day, students in schools around the world ask the question, "When am I ever going to use this in real life?" In *Instant Relevance,* author and keynote speaker Denis Sheeran equips you to create engaging lessons from experiences and events that matter to your students. Learn how to help your students see meaningful connections between the real world and what they learn in the classroom—because that's when learning sticks.

Escaping the School Leader's Dunk Tank

How to Prevail When Others Want to See You Drown

By Rebecca Coda and Rick Jetter
(@RebeccaCoda, @RickJetter)

No school leader is immune to the effects of discrimination, bad politics, revenge, or ego-driven coworkers. These kinds of dunk-tank situations can make an educator's life miserable. By sharing real-life stories and insightful research, the authors (who are dunk-tank survivors themselves) equip school leaders with the practical knowledge and emotional tools necessary to survive and, better yet, avoid getting "dunked."

Start. Right. Now.

Teaching and Leading for Excellence
By Todd Whitaker, Jeff Zoul,
and Jimmy Casas
(@ToddWhitaker, @Jeff_Zoul, @casas_jimmy)

In their work leading up to *Start. Right. Now.* Todd Whitaker, Jeff Zoul, and Jimmy Casas studied educators from across the nation and discovered four key behaviors of excellence: Excellent leaders and teachers Know the Way, Show the Way, Go the Way, and Grow Each Day. If you are ready to take the first step toward excellence, this motivating book will put you on the right path.

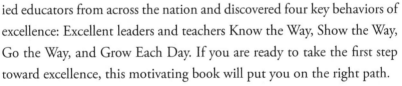

About the Authors

Shelley Burgess has served as an award-winning teacher, principal, Director of Student Achievement, and Assistant Superintendent of Educational Leadership. Her highly respected work focuses on building leadership capacity through coaching, collaboration, and building a positive culture of change which leads to dramatic improvements in teaching and learning. She now works as a full-time partner in Dave Burgess Consulting, Inc. and is the coauthor of *P is for PIRATE: Inspirational ABC's for Educators.*

Beth Houf is the proud principal at Fulton Middle School in central Missouri. She is passionate about developing schools that encourage high levels of learning and empowerment for all. In addition to her role as principal, she also serves as a facilitator for the Missouri Department of Elementary and Secondary Education's Leadership Academy, providing monthly training to state educational leaders. Beth was named a Missouri Exemplary New Principal in 2011 and the Missouri National Distinguished Principal for 2016.